A Practical Introduction to Pascal

Macmillan Computer Science Series

Consulting Editor

Professor F. H. Sumner, University of Manchester

G. M. Birtwistle, *Discrete Event Modelling on Simula*

Richard Bornat, *Understanding and Writing Compilers*

J. K. Buckle, *The ICL 2900 Series*

Derek Coleman, *A Structured Programming Approach to Data**

Andrew J. T. Colin, *Programming and Problem-solving in Algol 68**

S. M. Deen, *Fundamentals of Data Base Systems**

J. B. Gosling, *Design of Arithmetic Units for Digital Computers*

David Hopkin and Barbara Moss, *Automata**

H. Kopetz, *Software Reliability*

A. Learner and A. J. Powell, *An Introduction to Algol 68 through Problems**

A. M. Lister, *Fundamentals of Operating Systems, second edition**

Brian Meek, *Fortran, PL/I and the Algols*

Derrick Morris and Roland N. Ibbett, *The MU5 Computer System*

John Race, *Case Studies in Systems Analysis*

I. R. Wilson and A. M. Addyman, *A Practical Introduction to Pascal*

*The titles marked with an asterisk were prepared during the Consulting Editorship of Professor J. S. Rohl, University of Western Australia.

A Practical Introduction to Pascal

I. R. Wilson
A. M. Addyman

*Department of Computer Science,
University of Manchester*

First edition 1978
Reprinted 1979 (twice)

Published by
THE MACMILLAN PRESS LTD
London and Basingstoke
Associated companies in Delhi Dublin
Hong Kong Johannesburg Lagos Melbourne
New York Singapore and Tokyo

Typeset in 10/12 Press Roman by
Reproduction Drawings Ltd, Sutton, Surrey
and printed in Great Britain by
Unwin Brothers Limited
The Gresham Press Old Woking Surrey
A member of the Staples Printing Group

British Library Cataloguing in Publication Data

Wilson, I R
    A practical introduction to Pascal.–(Macmillan
    computer science series).
    1. PASCAL (Computer program language)
    I. Title II. Addyman, A M
    001.6 424   QA76.73.P/

    ISBN 0–333–23582–7

---

to
Alleyn, Fiona
Hilary, Rebecca and Sarah

Contents

Preface

The popularity of Pascal as a teaching language has rapidly increased, as demonstrated by Addyman's survey conducted over all European and American institutions (*Comput. Bull.,* Series 2, 8, June 1976, 31). This is due both to the desirable features of the language and to the ease of producing an efficient compiler. As an instance of the latter, the authors have investigated the full CDC CYBER compiler and found it to throughput at 1.8 times the rate of the manufacturer's Fortran compiler.

These features of the language and compilers have also been favourably regarded by system programmers and users of microprocessors. In the latter field, it is the belief of the authors that Pascal will supersede the programming language BASIC.

Specifically, undergraduates in the Department of Computer Science at Manchester University program largely in Pascal. An introductory lecture course on basic programming techniques, given at Manchester, has been taken as a basis for this book. In addition to lectures, the course consists of two kinds of practical session. The first is based on the solution of short pencil-and-paper exercises. The second requires the student to write complete programs and run them in an 'edit and go' mode on interactive computer terminals. Each chapter of the book concludes with exercises and problems suitable for these purposes. Although solutions to all of these are not presented in the book, teaching staff may obtain them by application to the authors.

The full Pascal language is presented in a practical manner, with reference to example applications. Indeed, the importance of the design of data structures as well as an algorithm to solve a problem is recognised by devoting seven chapters to this area. It is hoped that the book will be of use to first-course students and to more experienced programmers not yet familiar with Pascal.

Thus the purpose of the book is to provide an introduction to programming and not to act as a definitive reference work. The latter role is currently fulfilled by K. Jensen and N. Wirth, *Pascal-User Manual and Report* (Springer-Verlag, New York, 1975).

The stepwise refinement technique of program design and development is both used and advocated. However, specific diagrammatic representations (such as structure charts, tree diagrams, flowcharts, etc.) in combination with this book are not precluded.

The authors wish to acknowledge the assistance and encouragement of colleagues, in particular Dr C. C. Kirkham, Dr J. Rushby and Professor F. H. Sumner. They also wish to thank Miss J. Scrivens for her patient typing, and Professor D. Barron of Southampton University, for reviewing the manuscript.

The syntax diagrams which appear in the book were drawn with the assistance of the Manchester University Computer Graphics Unit. The program examples were printed on a DIABLO printer attached to the MU5 research computer.

University of Manchester,   I. R. WILSON
March 1978   A. M. ADDYMAN

1 Introduction

A computer is an electronic machine which is capable of performing accurate calculations and movements of information, reliably and at high speed (typically one million per second). It can execute repetitive tasks as combinations of the simple 'instructions' which it stores and understands. These instructions relate to calculations on, and movements of, numbers in the computer's memory or 'store'—comparisons of the numbers—and directions as to which instruction to do next. The computer is thus a suitable tool for the solution of problems which are well defined, involve large numbers of calculations and/or process large volumes of information. Applications vary from calculations of flight paths to automating all banking transactions.

It is possible to solve a problem on a computer, by inserting into it a set of numbers representing the 'data' of the problem and a suitable combination of computer instructions. However, this is a tedious and error-prone task. Problems are solved on a computer by preparing the solution in one of many programming languages. These permit the solution to be specified with brevity and clarity to the human user, while avoiding the lack of precision and the ambiguity of the English language. For example, is 'time flies' a remark or a command? Such a prepared solution is called a 'program' and the act of preparation is called 'programming'. A good program should reflect the nature of the problem and the steps involved in its solution. These steps, however expressed, are called an 'algorithm' and this book is concerned with the expression of algorithms in the language Pascal.

Pascal was invented in 1970 by Professor Niklaus Wirth of Zurich. It was named after the famous mathematician Blaise Pascal, who invented one of the earliest practical calculators. The language permits the structure and detail of a program solution to be expressed in terms of the information to be processed and the actions to be performed. Indeed, the ease of specifying the structure of the solution can make problem-solving in Pascal simpler and more elegant than in 'older' computer languages, such as Fortran, Algol and BASIC.

In general, the process of using a computer to solve a problem involves some organisation. Seven steps can be distinguished as follows.

(1) Understand the nature of the problem, in terms of the information available, the information to be produced and any assumptions to be made. A detailed enquiry should be made on these points before proceeding. The information available will constitute the 'input' or 'data' to the program. The form, units, limiting values and the amount of data, will affect the design of the program. The information to be produced will constitute the 'output' from the program. Care should be taken to ensure that this gives the required items of information, in the form and units required.

(2) Determine the actions required to perform the solution and the type/amount
of information to be stored in the computer during the solution. The design
of an algorithm and associated 'data structures' is a critical part of problem-
solving. Computer efficiency, correct solution of the complete problem,
clarity and the ability to make later modifications, may all be considered.
Specialised techniques are available to assist in this task, but the beginner is
advised to take the advice in this book as to good practice.

(3) Write or 'code' the specification of the stored information and actions, in
Pascal.

(4) Prepare the written program and its data, in a form readable by the computer. Special typing devices exist to do this. Some are connected directly to
the computer and are said to be 'on line'. Others produce rolls of paper tape
or rectangular cards with holes punched to represent each character. These
paper tapes or punched cards are fed to the computer via fast 'input
devices'.

(5) Command the computer to convert the Pascal program into computer instructions and to obey these instructions. These two processes are called
'compilation' and 'running' of a program. Compilation is carried out by a
special program already within the computer called a 'compiler'. The
commands to compile, obtain previously stored data, etc., are usually
written as 'job control statements' at the head of the program. Each computer has a different notation for job control statements, and local documentation must be consulted before writing them.

(6) The execution of a program by the computer will, assuming there are no
errors (see 7), produce the results. These may appear on an 'output device',
such as the on-line terminal into which the program was typed, or a 'line
printer'. The latter prints a line at a time, at high speed (one thousand per
minute, say). The results may be examined for correctness.

(7) Should the solutions produce the required information, no further action is
needed. However, the complexity of problems tackled for computer solution
and the organisation required to produce a correct unambiguous program,
make this unlikely at first attempt. Removing errors from a program is
called 'debugging'. The errors may arise because the program is not accepted
by the compiler as correct Pascal. These are referred to as 'compile time
errors'. Alternatively, the errors may be 'run time errors' which may occur
when the computer 'obeys' (or executes) the solution. A deliberate effort should
be made to find as many such errors as possible, by 'testing' the solution on
difficult (correct and faulty) data.

For a program to be correct Pascal it must at least correspond to the defined
'syntax' of the language. Pascal syntax is presented as 'syntax diagrams' which
show the permissible alternatives for each part of each kind of sentence and
where the parts may appear. Some of these diagrams appear in the body of the
book, and the complete set is given in appendix I. As an example of their use,

personal name

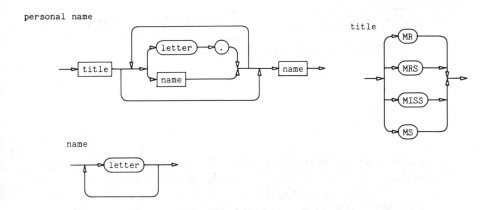

Figure 1.1

the diagrams in figure 1.1 describe all normally used forms of personal name. Rectangular boxes enclose objects defined elsewhere and round-ended boxes enclose actual characters which must appear or objects requiring no further definition. Note that 'title' has several possible forms and that a surname may be preceded by zero, one or more initials and/or forenames.

The reader may find it helpful to test his understanding of the material in each chapter by attempting to reproduce the complete programs given in the text. A comment at the top of each program or description in the text defines the problem solved. Should a comparison of his attempt with the solution given prove satisfactory, the exercises and programming tasks given at the end of each chapter may be attempted.

Exercise

Use syntax diagrams to describe all shopping-list items of the form shown in the following example. You may assume that a limited number of different types of goods exist.

4 lbs potatoes	£0.47
2 oz garlic	£0.15
5 apples	£0.30

2 The Form of a Program and Basic Calculations

2.1 The Style of Writing in Pascal

A Pascal program may be considered as a series of 'statements' or rules which the computer must follow step by step. These statements are written in a notation which resembles a restricted form of English and algebra. The restrictions are that only a small number of different forms of statement are provided and that the vocabulary used is limited. This vocabulary consists of keywords with fixed meanings called 'delimiters' (for example, **IF**, **BEGIN**, **END**), names of objects or 'identifiers' (for example, COST, SEX) and other symbols (+ − .).

Identifiers are usually specified and given a meaning by the programmer. Each must begin with a letter, which may be followed by any combination of letters and digits. It may be of any length, but should differ from all other identifiers in the first eight characters. Further, none of the delimiter words should be used as identifiers. A complete list of delimiters is given in appendix II. Thus

Legal Identifiers	Illegal/Inadvisable Identifiers	
CUSTOMER	CUSTOMERCOUNT	(first 8 same)
A	MAX TEMP	(space)
A1B2	X − 1	(minus)
VERYLENGTHYIDENTIFIER	IF	(delimiter)

Any number of spaces and/or newlines may be used to separate the words and symbols in a Pascal statement. However, each statement must be specifically separated from the next, if any, by a ; symbol.

2.2 The General Form of a Program

The over-all written form of a Pascal program is determined from the syntax diagram of the program, as shown in figure 2.1. Thus each program has a name, a bracketed set of names concerned with data and results, and is terminated by a full stop. The examples used here (until chapter 8) will have a first line of the form

PROGRAM name of program (INPUT, OUTPUT);

The set of 'declarations' required by the syntax diagram specifies the names and properties of identifiers to be used.

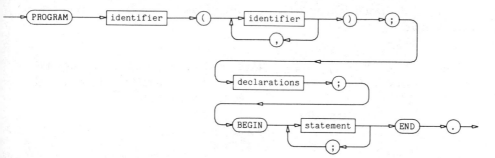

Figure 2.1

2.3 The Assignment Statement and Simple Arithmetic

The basic calculations made in a Pascal program are applied to 'variables' and 'constants'. Constants are constant in value and may be written (among other forms—see section 2.4 and chapter 4) in normal arithmetic number style, without commas or spaces. For example, 4 or 3.1

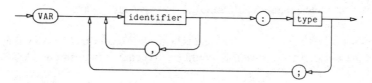

Figure 2.2

Variables are identifiers which may be given a value and which may be altered in value as the program is obeyed. They are specified in the **VAR** declaration as identifiers of some type (see figure 2.2). Initially, only the types INTEGER and REAL will be considered. An example† is

```
VAR  A,B,C  :  INTEGER;
     R,S     :  REAL;
```

which specifies or 'declares' five identifiers—A, B, C of type INTEGER and R, S of type REAL. INTEGER variables may only take a whole number value . . . −1, 0, 1, 2 . . . . REAL variables may take a value with a fractional part, for example, −0.1 or 13.25.

A variable may be given a value using the 'assignment statement', in which

† In these examples, the delimiter words such as **VAR** are in bold type merely to increase clarity.

the variable is followed by the 'assignment operator' := and a calculation. For example

```
A  :=  1
```

gives the value 1 to A. This is *not* a mathematical identity, because it does not mean that A is always the same as 1. The statement is a rule the computer will follow, if directed to execute it. The rule says 'whatever value (if any) A had before, now give A the value 1'.

The calculation after the := symbol may involve variables. For example.

```
A  :=  B
```

gives A the same value as B. The variable B is not altered in the process. A series of variables and/or constants may appear in a calculation or 'expression', by separating each of them with an appropriate algebraic symbol, for example, $+ - * /$ and brackets. When dividing two integers the delimiter word **DIV** is used.

These symbols are known as 'operators' and a fuller description of the available operators and their use appears in chapter 4. An example is

```
C  :=  A + B
```

This causes the computer to obtain the value previously assigned to A, add to it the value previously assigned to B and place the result in C.

2.4 A Complete Program with Simple Input/Output

Consider the trivial problem of adding two given integers and printing the result. A complete program to solve this would be that shown in example 2A.

Example 2A

```
PROGRAM EX2A(INPUT,OUTPUT);
VAR A,B,C :INTEGER;
BEGIN
READ (A,B);
C  := A+B;
WRITELN (C)
END.
```

The statements on lines 4 and 6 require some explanation. The READ statement is used to specify that successive values are to be taken from the data and assigned to the variables given after in brackets. Each value read is real if the variable is REAL and integer if the variable is INTEGER. The WRITELN statement specifies that the calculated value of each expression given inside the brackets is, in turn, printed on the output from the computer. Here, only one simple expression (C) is given. After all of the values are printed by a WRITELN, the output moves to the start of the next line.

Unless otherwise specified (see chapter 3), the statements in the program are

executed from left to right and top to bottom. Thus program EX2A takes two
integer numbers from the data, assigns them to A and B respectively, adds these
two values together, places the answer in C, and prints the value of C on the
output.

2.5 Readable Programs

In addition to choosing meaningful identifiers and laying out the program
neatly, three simple means are provided to make programs more readable. The
first is the use of 'comments'. This is English text surrounded by { and } symbols.
A comment may appear between any two symbols anywhere in a program, may
cover several lines and appear in the middle of a statement, but may not contain
the symbol}. All comments are ignored by the Pascal compiler and are used to
amplify and explain the program to a human reader. Many computers do not
have the curly bracket symbols, in which case (* and *) are used instead. For
example

```
(* THIS IS
   A COMMENT *)
```

The second aid to readability concerns the use of quantities which have a
special meaning, but nevertheless do not change in value throughout the program. These constants may be given a name or identifier, which is used in place
of the constant wherever it appears. The identifier and associated constant value
are specified in a **CONST** declaration, which must appear before the **VAR**
declaration (see figure 2.3). For example the declaration

CONST INCREMENT = 3

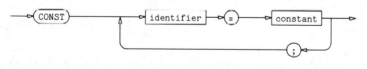

Figure 2.3

permits the identifier INCREMENT to be used in place of the number 3.

The third means of improving readability concerns the output of results. In
addition to numbers, the WRITELN statement permits text to be printed, by
giving the text enclosed in ' symbols. Thus if the trivial problem were to read
two numbers (not necessarily integer) and to print their sum plus a fixed increment, the solution might be as shown in example 2B. The identifiers here have
been chosen to correspond to a particular application. Note also that it is
assumed that the input and output to the program are at the same 'terminal'
device. If they are not, the output would be improved by printing out the
numbers read in.

Example 2B

```
(* CALCULATE CAR RUNNING COSTS *)
PROGRAM EX2B(INPUT,OUTPUT);
CONST ROADTAX = 50.0;
VAR GARAGEBILL,INSURANCE,TOTAL : REAL;
BEGIN
READ(GARAGEBILL,INSURANCE);
TOTAL := GARAGEBILL + INSURANCE + ROADTAX;
WRITELN('TOTAL COST IS' , TOTAL)
END.
```

It is good practice to make a program readable, because it assists 'debugging', testing and later modification.

Exercises

2.1 Which of the following identifiers are legal in Pascal?

X, X1, 1X, X1X, TEMPERATURE, JOHN BROWN, RE-ACTIVATE, TEMPERATE, ANTIDISESTABLISHMENTARIANISM, X(3), BEGIN, CASE

2.2 The following program is not intended to be meaningful, but it is also not correct Pascal. Correct all of the errors.

```
PROGRAM INDEX(INPUT,OUTPUT)
VAR I,J : INTEGER;
    R   : REAL;
BEGIN
J := 3.4;
READ(I, K, R)
R + J := R;
WRITELN (I, J, K, R)
END
```

2.3 What are the guiding rules for writing readable programs. Rewrite program EX2A to follow these rules.

Problem

Write a program to read in a temperature in centigrade units and print it out in Fahrenheit units. The program should include two named constants.

3 Basic Control Constructs

A problem of sufficient complexity to require the use of a computer for its solution is not likely to be solved by a succession of simple calculations. Indeed, if the computer is to behave as anything other than a fast calculating machine, it must, at various points in a solution, be directed to take some step other than that immediately following.

Consider the calculation of the income tax to be paid by each of the employees of a company. This male chauvinistic problem might be further specified as

Information available	:	earnings, number of dependants, expenses, type of employee (1–man, 2–woman, 3–boy)
Information required	:	amount of tax
Special cases	:	none should pay negative tax and a compulsory works charity contribution depends on employee type (£5, £2 or £1)
Inbuilt assumptions	:	rate of tax is 35% and a £150 tax-free allowance is made for each dependant; expenses and the charity contribution are tax deductible

The solution in Pascal is given later in this chapter, but the problem is given here to illustrate a requirement to choose the next solution step at any point. Three different calculations of charity levy may be selected. Two different directions have to be chosen, for employees whose allowances are greater than their income (zero tax) and for those whose income is greater than their allowances. Furthermore, all of the steps in the solution are to be repeated for every one of the employees.

In fact, Pascal provides directly for three situations in which the solution steps are not consecutive. These are *repetition*; *choice* of one of two different actions and *selection* of one of many different actions. The Pascal statements used in the construction of programs where control is exercised over the actions taken, are called 'control constructs'. This chapter is devoted to them.

3.1 Repetition

Even the solution of a simple problem, such as performing the calculation given in chapter 2 for 100 different data pairs, would be laborious, if every calculation had to be written out

```
    .
    .
READ(A,B);
C := A + B;
WRITELN('THE SUM IS', C);
READ(A,B);
C := A + B;
WRITELN('THE SUM IS', C);
READ(A,B);
    .
    .
    .
```

In Pascal, this is avoided by grouping together the statements to be repeated and specifying how often they are to be repeated. Three ways are provided to do this.

3.1.1 UNTIL Some Condition is Satisfied

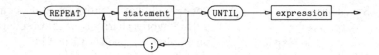

Figure 3.1

This type of statement uses the words **REPEAT** and **UNTIL** to group the statements to be repeated (see figure 3.1). The statements are repeated **UNTIL** the expression at the end is true. A more detailed discussion of this type of expression is given in chapter 4. It will suffice here to say that two calculations may be compared using the symbols

$$<, <=, =, <>, >=, >$$

where $<>$ means not equal. In example 3A, two statements are repeated until it is true, after obeying them, that the variable NUMBER is zero.

Example 3A

```
(* ADD INTEGERS TILL ONE IS ZERO *)
PROGRAM EX3A(INPUT,OUTPUT);
VAR SUM,NUMBER :INTEGER;
BEGIN
SUM := 0;
REPEAT
     READ (NUMBER);
     SUM := SUM + NUMBER
UNTIL NUMBER = 0;
WRITELN ('THE TOTAL IS', SUM)
END.
```

Note: **REPEAT** loops must be obeyed *at least once*.

3.1.2 WHILE Some Condition Remains Satisfied

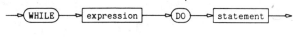

Figure 3.2

In this kind of loop, the controlling expression is written between the words **WHILE** and **DO** (see figure 3.2). While it is true before the *single* statement is obeyed, the repetition continues. Should it be required to repeat several statements, these are grouped together into a single 'compound statement', by surrounding them with the words **BEGIN** and **END** (see figure 3.3). It is good practice to indent a compound statement, by starting each line of it with some spaces (typically 2 to 5).

```
compound statement
```

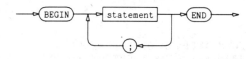

Figure 3.3

Example 3B calculates the largest power of one number, which is less than or equal to another number. For example, the two numbers 10 and 3 give the answer 2, since $3^2 = 9 \leqslant 10$ but $3^3 = 27 > 10$.

Example 3B
```
(* A >= B↑N , FIND LARGEST N *)
PROGRAM EX3B(INPUT,OUTPUT);
VAR A,B,PRODUCT :REAL;
    POWER        :INTEGER;
BEGIN
READ (A,B);
POWER := 0; PRODUCT := B;
WHILE PRODUCT <= A DO
    BEGIN
    POWER := POWER + 1;
    PRODUCT := PRODUCT * B
    END;
WRITELN ('LARGEST POWER OF', B, ' <', A, ' IS', POWER)
END.
```

Note: The **WHILE** form of repetition is most useful when the loop is *not* to be obeyed *at all* in some circumstances. For example, 3 and 10 should give the answer 0 in the above program, since $10^0 = 1 \leqslant 3$ and $10^1 = 10 > 3$. Does the program do this?

3.1.3 FOR a Known Number of Times

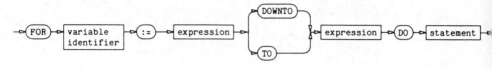

Figure 3.4

In some repetitions it may be known or calculated in advance how many times
the statements are to be performed. A **FOR** type of loop is obeyed for every
value of a variable from some starting value to (and including) some ending
value (see figure 3.4). This variable is called the *control variable*. The starting
and ending values of the control variable are given as calculations. A high value
DOWNTO a lower value or a low value **TO** a higher value may be specified.

In example 3C, a compound statement is again used to group two statements
as one. The compound statement is obeyed for I equal to 1, 2, 3 . . . N (that is,
N times).

Example 3C

```
(* FORM AVERAGE OF N NUMBERS *)
PROGRAM EX3C(INPUT,OUTPUT);
VAR I,N                 :INTEGER;
    AVERAGE,SUM,NUMBER  :REAL;
BEGIN
READ(N); SUM := 0;
FOR I := 1 TO N DO
    BEGIN
    READ(NUMBER);
    SUM := SUM + NUMBER
    END;
AVERAGE := SUM / N;
WRITELN('AVERAGE IS', AVERAGE)
END.
```

Notes: (a) A **FOR** loop is not obeyed at all if the starting value is greater (less
for **DOWNTO**) than the ending value.
(b) The control variable, the starting value and the ending value should not be
altered within the loop. They should all be of the same type (often integer but
see chapters 4 and 7) but must not be real.
(c) The final value of the control variable is undefined after a normal exit from
a **FOR** loop.

3.1.4 Nested Loops

In Pascal, each control construct forms a single statement. Thus it is possible to
include any one as part of another. In particular, a repeated statement or compound statement may itself be repeated. Two examples, 3D and 3E, demon-

strate this. The first is a modification of program EX3C to cope with M groups of numbers. The second calculates, from two given integers, the largest integer which divides exactly into both (called their highest common factor or HCF). This uses the facts that the HCF must also divide exactly into the difference of the two numbers and that if the numbers are equal then the HCF is also that value.

Example 3D

```
(* FORM AVERAGE OF EACH OF M GROUPS OF NUMBERS *)
PROGRAM EX3D(INPUT,OUTPUT);
VAR I,J,M,N                :INTEGER;
    AVERAGE,SUM,NUMBER :REAL;
BEGIN
READ(M);
FOR J := 1 TO M DO
    BEGIN
    READ(N); SUM := 0;
    FOR I := 1 TO N DO
        BEGIN
        READ(NUMBER);
        SUM := SUM + NUMBER
        END;
    AVERAGE := SUM / N;
    WRITELN('AVERAGE IS', AVERAGE)
    END
END.
```

Example 3E

```
(* FIND HCF OF TWO NOS *)
PROGRAM EX3E(INPUT,OUTPUT);
VAR A,B :INTEGER;
BEGIN
READ (A,B);
REPEAT
    WHILE A > B DO A := A-B;
    WHILE B > A DO B := B-A
UNTIL A = B;
WRITELN ('HCF IS', A)
END.
```

3.2 Choice—The IF Statement

The nature of a problem may be such that some step must or must not be taken, or such that one of two different steps must be taken, at some point. The Pascal **IF** statement is used to cope with these situations (see figure 3.5).

Figure 3.5

The expression controlling the choice may be *true*, in which case the first statement is obeyed, or *false*, in which case the second, if any, is obeyed. Two examples, 3F and 3G, illustrate a choice of whether or not to obey a statement and a choice of two different statements to obey.

Example 3F

```
(* FIND MAXIMUM OF N NOS *)
PROGRAM EX3F(INPUT,OUTPUT);
VAR N,MAXNO,NUMBER,I :INTEGER;
BEGIN
READ(N);
READ(MAXNO);
FOR I := 1 TO N-1 DO
     BEGIN
     READ(NUMBER);
     IF NUMBER > MAXNO THEN MAXNO := NUMBER
     END;
WRITELN('THE MAX NO. IS', MAXNO)
END.
```

Example 3G

```
(* COUNT HOW MANY POSITIVE
   AND HOW MANY NEGATIVE NUMBERS *)
PROGRAM EX3G(INPUT,OUTPUT);
VAR POSCOUNT,NEGCOUNT :INTEGER;
    NUMBER            :REAL;
BEGIN
POSCOUNT := 0;
NEGCOUNT := 0;
REPEAT
     READ(NUMBER);
     IF NUMBER >= 0 THEN
          POSCOUNT := POSCOUNT + 1
     ELSE NEGCOUNT := NEGCOUNT + 1
UNTIL NUMBER = 0  (*LAST NUMBER ZERO*);
WRITELN('THERE WERE', POSCOUNT, ' POSITIVE NUMBERS');
WRITELN('AND', NEGCOUNT, ' NEGATIVE NUMBERS')
END.
```

In example 3F, the statement MAXNO := NUMBER is only obeyed if NUMBER is greater than MAXNO. In example 3G, one of the two different counts is incremented, depending on whether the number is positive or negative. Note that there is no semicolon before the **ELSE** in example 3G, because the **ELSE** section is part of the **IF** statement.

Any type of Pascal statement may appear in either the **THEN** or **ELSE** section of an **IF** statement. Should a further choice of step be required, an **IF** statement may appear. A compound statement may be used if the choice affects a group of statements.

In example 3H, the two situations of a zero and a non-zero value are distinguished. In the latter case, a further distinction is made between a positive and a negative value.

Example 3H

```
(* FORM SEPARATE TOTALS OF POSITIVE AND NEGATIVE NOS
   AND COUNT HOW MANY ZEROS *)
PROGRAM EX3H(INPUT,OUTPUT);
VAR I,N,NUMBER,POSITIVESUM,NEGATIVESUM,COUNT :INTEGER;
BEGIN
READ(N);
POSITIVESUM := 0;
NEGATIVESUM := 0;
COUNT := 0;
FOR I := 1 TO N DO
     BEGIN
     READ(NUMBER);
     IF NUMBER = 0 THEN
          COUNT := COUNT + 1
     ELSE IF NUMBER > 0 THEN
               POSITIVESUM := POSITIVESUM + NUMBER
          ELSE NEGATIVESUM := NEGATIVESUM + NUMBER
     END;
WRITELN('TOTAL OF POSITIVE NOS IS', POSITIVESUM);
WRITELN('TOTAL OF NEGATIVE NOS IS', NEGATIVESUM);
WRITELN('AND THE NUMBER OF ZEROS IS', COUNT)
END.
```

In this example, an **IF** statement appears as the **ELSE** part of an **IF** statement. However, where it appears as the **THEN** part, some doubt over the meaning may be resolved by noting that the innermost statement is the first to be completed when the program is read by the computer. Thus

```
IF A <> 0 THEN
     IF A > 0 THEN
          P := Q
     ELSE P := R
```

gives P the value of R when A is negative and no action is taken if A is zero.

3.3   Selection—the CASE Statement

A solution may need to take one of many different enumerated steps. In this case, each step in the solution is given one or more constant values and all the steps are included in a **CASE** statement (see figure 3.6). An expression is given,

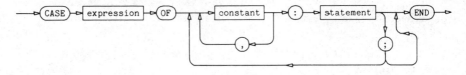

Figure 3.6

whose value determines which step to select, each time the **CASE** statement is obeyed. This expression and the constant values should all be of the same type (often integer, but see chapter 4) and must not be real.

In example 3I, a number between 1 and 7 is read in and converted on output to the word for the appropriate day of the week, MONDAY, TUESDAY, etc.

Example 3I

```
(* READ NO, PRINT DAY OF WEEK *)
PROGRAM EX3I(INPUT,OUTPUT);
VAR DAYNO :INTEGER;
BEGIN
READ(DAYNO);
CASE DAYNO OF
   1: WRITELN('MONDAY');
   2: WRITELN('TUESDAY');
   3: WRITELN('WEDNESDAY');
   4: WRITELN('THURSDAY');
   5: WRITELN('FRIDAY');
   6: WRITELN('SATURDAY');
   7: WRITELN('SUNDAY')
END (*OF CASE*)
END.
```

When DAYNO is 1, only the statement with the value 1: is selected. When DAYNO is 2, the statement with the value 2: is selected, etc.

Notes: (a) By suitable choice of data structure (see chapters 7 and 10), it is often possible to reduce a complete case statement to one action. However, where the selection is from significantly different actions the case statement is a useful construct.

(b) If the value of the selection expression is not one of the constant case values, a fault message will be printed and the program will fail.

3.4 Representing Other Control Constructs

The difficulty of correcting and amending computer programs is such that clarity is all important in writing them. Pascal aids this by providing the control constructs described above, and these should be used wherever possible. However, some problem solutions would have to be artificially reformulated to fit into the pattern of the given constructs. The two most common of these situations are where

(1) a loop of steps is exited not from the top (WHILE) or bottom (UNTIL) but from an intermediate point;
(2) in the middle of a nested set of constructs, an exit to some outer level is required, for example, if a fault situation is encountered.

These problems are overcome by use of the GOTO statement, which causes the computer to jump directly to another statement of the program. This statement is marked by labelling it with a number and colon written before the statement. For example

```
        GOTO 123;
        .
        .
    123: (* GOTO JUMPS HERE *)
```

The label must be declared *before* the CONSTant declarations using the LABEL declaration, as shown in figure 3.7. The GOTO statement most often appears as the THEN part of a conditional statement. Examples 3J and 3K illustrate this.

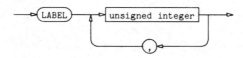

Figure 3.7

Example 3J

```
(* ADD NOS TILL -1 *)
PROGRAM EX3J(INPUT,OUTPUT);
LABEL 123;
VAR SUM,NUMBER :INTEGER;
BEGIN
SUM := 0;
WHILE TRUE DO
      BEGIN
      READ(NUMBER);
      IF NUMBER = -1 THEN GOTO 123;
      SUM := SUM + NUMBER
      END;
123: (* JUMP HERE WHEN -1 READ *)
WRITELN('THE SUM IS', SUM)
END.
```

Example 3K

```
(* FORM AVERAGE OF EACH OF M GROUPS OF NUMBERS
    STOPPING IF A NEGATIVE NUMBER IS ENCOUNTERED *)
PROGRAM EX3K(INPUT,OUTPUT);
LABEL 33;
VAR I,J,M,N                 :INTEGER;
    AVERAGE,SUM,NUMBER  :REAL;
BEGIN
READ(M);
FOR J := 1 TO M DO
    BEGIN
    READ(N); SUM := 0;
    FOR I := 1 TO N DO
        BEGIN
        READ(NUMBER);
        IF NUMBER < 0 THEN GOTO 33;
        SUM := SUM + NUMBER
        END;
    AVERAGE := SUM / N;
    WRITELN('AVERAGE IS', AVERAGE)
    END;
33: (* JUMP HERE IF NEGATIVE NUM FOUND *)
END.
```

Notes: (a) The first example above could arguably be written as a **WHILE** loop with the READ statement repeated prior to the loop. Whether this is justified (in this case it is) depends on how many steps are repeated and whether the first time round the loop is special in some way.

(b) A program containing **GOTO** statements has a greater need of comments.

(c) **END** is not a statement. Thus if a label is placed on an **END**, it is considered to be on an empty statement preceding the **END**. Hence the previous statement must be terminated by a semicolon. Empty statements (that is, redundant ; symbols) may appear wherever a statement may be used.

3.5   Advice on Problem-solving

The examples up to this point have all been presented complete. However, when larger and more complex problems are tackled, it may not be possible abstractly to conceive of the complete solution in Pascal. Indeed, this may initially be true of the short exercises in this chapter.

This difficulty may be overcome by evolving the Pascal program from a general statement of the solution. This statement may be broken down into a series of steps until each step is sufficiently explicit. Before each step is refined it must be categorised as follows.

(1) Direct action (assignment, read, write)
(2) Repetition (**WHILE, FOR, REPEAT**)
(3) Choice (**IF**)

(4) Selection (**CASE**)

(5) Series of simpler steps (compound statement)

This technique is called 'stepwise refinement'.

Consider the tax problem posed earlier. Example 3L—first stage might be made as a general statement. The number of employees is read into N and N repetitions of some process solve the problem.

Example 3L—First Stage

```
(* TAX CALCULATION FIRST STAGE *)
PROGRAM EX3L(INPUT,OUTPUT);
VAR I,N :INTEGER;
BEGIN
READ(N);
FOR I := 1 TO N DO
      process data for 1 employee
END.
```

Concentrate now on the process for one employee. Because several calculations have to be made, a compound statement is chosen and example 3L—second stage might result.

Example 3L—Second Stage

```
(* TAX CALCULATION SECOND STAGE *)
PROGRAM EX3L(INPUT,OUTPUT);
VAR I,N :INTEGER;
BEGIN
READ(N);
FOR I := 1 TO N DO
      BEGIN
      read data for 1 employee
      calculate charity levy
      calculate total expenses
      calculate allowance
      calculate tax
      print tax owing
      END
END.
```

Each of the steps in our one-employee process may be made more explicit by considering which type of Pascal statement is to be used. Where only a direct action is involved, it may now hopefully be written fully in Pascal. Otherwise a further refinement may be necessary. Example 3L—third stage represents progress so far.

Example 3L—Third Stage

```
(* TAX CALCULATION THIRD STAGE *)
PROGRAM EX3L(INPUT,OUTPUT);
CONST ALLOWANCEPER = 150;
VAR TAX,INCOME,EXPENSES,ALLOW,CHARITYLEVY :REAL;
    I,N,DEPENDENTS,EMPLTYPE                :INTEGER;
BEGIN
READ(N);
FOR I := 1 TO N DO
    BEGIN
    READ(INCOME,EXPENSES,DEPENDENTS,EMPLTYPE);
    CASE EMPLTYPE OF
      1: men
      2: women
      3: boys
    END;
    EXPENSES := EXPENSES + CHARITYLEVY;
    ALLOW := ALLOWANCEPER*DEPENDENTS + EXPENSES;
    IF INCOME > ALLOW THEN
        calculate tax
    ELSE zero tax
    WRITELN('TAX FOR EMPLOYEE', I, ' IS', TAX)
    END
END.
```

Because each of the steps not now explicit is an assignment, the complete solution follows directly and might be example 3L—final program.

Example 3L—Final Program

```
(* TAX CALCULATION FINAL PROGRAM *)
PROGRAM EX3L(INPUT,OUTPUT);
CONST ALLOWANCEPER = 150;
      RATE         = 0.35;
VAR TAX,INCOME,EXPENSES,ALLOW,CHARITYLEVY :REAL;
    I,N,DEPENDENTS,EMPLTYPE                :INTEGER;
BEGIN
READ(N);
FOR I := 1 TO N DO
    BEGIN
    READ(INCOME,EXPENSES,DEPENDENTS,EMPLTYPE);
    CASE EMPLTYPE OF
      1: CHARITYLEVY := 5;
      2: CHARITYLEVY := 2;
      3: CHARITYLEVY := 1
    END;
    EXPENSES := EXPENSES + CHARITYLEVY;
    ALLOW := ALLOWANCEPER*DEPENDENTS + EXPENSES;
    IF INCOME > ALLOW THEN
        TAX := (INCOME-ALLOW) * RATE
    ELSE TAX := 0;
    WRITELN('TAX FOR EMPLOYEE', I, ' IS', TAX)
    END
END.
```

Note that as each section of explicit Pascal is written, the appropriate declarations **(VAR** and **CONST)** are added to the program.

Exercises

3.1 Write Pascal statement(s) to
(a) print the text 'ZERO' or 'NONZERO' depending on whether the variable PENCE is equal to zero or not;
(b) calculate the amount of tax payable £T for a given income of £I. You may assume that the first £200 are not taxed, the next £200 are taxed at 30% and the remainder at 40%. Further, the 40% rate is increased to 50% where the total income is greater than £5000.

3.2 Write a set of Pascal statements to read some positive integers, the last of which is zero, and to print the largest.

3.3 Consider animals boarding Noah's Ark. They are each given a punched card at the bottom of the gangplank. This card only has a number on it, being the animal category number, say, LION–1, TIGER–2, FLY–3, etc. Write a set of Pascal statements to read the numbers and print a boarding list of the animals which have come aboard. You may assume that the gangplank is raised when exactly 200 animals have boarded. For example

    LION
    FLY
    FLY
    TIGER
    LEOPARD
        .
        .
        .

Problems

3.1 Write a program to tabulate the values of the squares, cubes and factorials of all integers from 1 to 100.

3.2 Write a program to count the number of prime numbers less than 500. A prime number is a positive integer which does not divide exactly by any other positive integer. One technique (not by any means optimal) is to determine for each number whether it divides exactly by any number less than it.

4 Variables, Constants and Expressions

4.1 The Different Types of Variable and Constant

In previous chapters we have used only real and integer variables. There are, in fact, four standard scalar types of variable in Pascal—*integer, real, character* and *boolean*. Each type has its own forms of constant, its own operators (+, −, etc.) and its own 'standard functions'. These standard functions are named operations which may be applied to one value to yield another value. For example, one standard function is SQRT and SQRT (A) calculates from the value of the variable A the value of its square root.

An expression consists of a series of variables, constants, standard functions, other objects with a value (see later chapters) and intervening operators. Generally, these operators and objects are consistently of the same type. However, in some circumstances, values of one type may be used in an expression of another type.

This chapter is devoted to a practical description of expressions of these standard types. A further discussion of their properties is given in chapter 7.

4.2 The Precedence of Operators

The operators are given an order of importance or 'precedence' over each other. This specifies which operators are applied first when evaluating an expression. For example, * is more important (has a greater precedence) than + and hence a * operator is applied before a + operator. Thus

   1 + 2 * 3 has the value 7 not 9

If desired, this precedence may be overcome by use of brackets surrounding the section to be evaluated separately. Thus

   (1 + 2) * 3 has the value 9 not 7

The bracketed section has the form of an expression, and the rules of precedence also apply to this expression. Since two operators may not follow one another with no intervening value, only the first value in an expression may be negated. For example

   −A + B

Where other values are to be negated, brackets may be used to form a subexpression. For example

A * (−B)

Where operators have the same precedence, they are applied from left to right. Thus, since * and / have the same precedence

12 / 2 * 3 has the value 18 not 2

4.3 Real

The real operators are

+ −

and with greater precedence

* /

In general, a real constant may take the form shown in figure 4.1. For example

−2.13 0.1 2.1E9

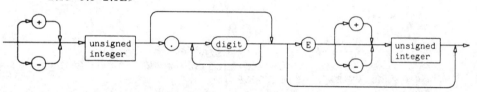

Figure 4.1

It is not permitted to write .1 or 1. as a constant or to include spaces or commas. The notation using the letter E is a convenience when writing very large or very small numbers. The integer following the E gives the number of decimal places right (or left if negative) to move the decimal point. Thus

2.1E9 is a shorthand for 2100000000
3.2E−7 is a shorthand for 0.00000032

It is also permitted, of course, to use the name of a declared **CONST** preceded by a + or −. However, only an unsigned constant may appear as an operand in an expression. Thus

A * −2.1 must be written as A * (−2.1)

Assuming R to be a real expression, standard functions which give a real value are

ABS(R) which yields the absolute value of R i.e.
ABS(R) is R if R is positive
ABS(R) is −R if R is negative

For example, ABS(2) is 2 and ABS(−2) is 2.

SQR(R)	which yields the value of the square of R
SQRT(R)	which yields the value of the square root of R
SIN(R) ⎫	which yield the trigonometric function
COS(R) ⎭	values of R, where R is measured in radians
ARCTAN(R)	which yields the principal value in radians of the arctan of R
LN(R)	which yields the natural logarithm of R (i.e. base e)
EXP(R)	which yields e raised to the power R

As an example of the use of real expressions, consider example 4A. This calculates the length of the third side of a triangle (C), given two sides (A and B) and the enclosed angle (W), according to the formula

$$C = \sqrt{(A^2 + B^2 - 2AB \cdot \text{cosine } W)}$$

The use of brackets round the expressions to which the functions are applied and the necessary * operators, should be noted in this example.

Example 4A

```
(* PRINT LENGTH OF THIRD SIDE OF TRIANGLE
   GIVEN TWO SIDES AND ENCLOSED ANGLE *)
PROGRAM EX4A(INPUT,OUTPUT);
VAR A,B,C,ANGLE :REAL;
BEGIN
READ (A,B,ANGLE);
C := SQRT(SQR(A) + SQR(B) - 2*A*B*COS(ANGLE));
WRITELN ('THE THIRD SIDE IS', C)
END.
```

Notes: (a) Real values can only be stored, by any given computer, to a limited number of significant figures (typically 5 to 15) and are only accurate to that extent. Thus two real values may not safely be compared for equality.
(b) Integer values (constants, variables and subexpressions) may be used in a real expression without qualification. The integer value is automatically converted to the corresponding real value.

4.4 Integer

The integer operators are

+ −

and with greater precedence

    ＊ DIV MOD

where **DIV** is division of non-negative integer values giving a truncated integer result and **MOD** gives the remainder. Thus

    A **MOD** B is A $-$ (A **DIV** B) ＊ B

For example

    15 **DIV** 4 is 3
    11 **MOD** 3 is 2

Thus the test of whether one integer divides another exactly (problem 3.2) could be

    M **DIV** N ＊ N = M

or

    M **MOD** N = 0

Integer constants have the normal arithmetic form and, in general, may be preceded by a + or $-$. However, as with real constants, only an unsigned constant may be used as an operand and no spaces or commas may be included.

    Assuming I to be an integer expression and R to be a real expression, standard functions which yield an integer value are

ABS(I)	which yields the absolute value of I, i.e.
	ABS(I) is I if I is positive
	ABS(I) is $-$I if I is negative
SQR(I)	which yields the value of the square of I
TRUNC(R)	which yields the whole part of R. The fractional part is discarded; for example
	TRUNC(1.9) is 1 TRUNC($-$1.9) is $-$1
ROUND(R)	which yields the integer nearest to R. However, should R be precisely 0.5 greater than some integer, it is rounded up if R is positive and down if R is negative. For example
	ROUND(3.1) is 3 ROUND(3.9) is 4
	ROUND($-$3.1) is $-$3 ROUND($-$3.9) is $-$4

    As an example of the use of integer standard functions, consider again the prime numbers problem. For a given number M, it is only necessary to examine for exact division those integers from $\sqrt{M}$ down to 2. Clearly, if M divides exactly by a larger integer (N) it must also divide by M **DIV** N which is smaller than $\sqrt{M}$. Thus, our starting point for examining M is the integer

```
ROUND(SQRT(M))
```

4.5 Character

Character variables are declared of type CHAR in the **VAR** declaration. For example

```
VAR C,D  :  CHAR;
```

Each variable may take the value of any one of the characters available on the computer on which the program is run. This varies with the computer character set used but the following may be assumed.

(1) For each character set, the characters are fixed and in a fixed order.
(2) The upper-case alphabet A . . Z is included, in that order and normally directly following one another.
(3) The decimal digits 0 . . 9 are included, in that order and directly following one another.
(4) The space character is included.

A character constant is represented by writing it enclosed in single quotes. A single quote itself is written twice. For example

```
'A'   'B'   '0'   '9'   ''''
```

No operators are available to perform calculations on character values, but they may be compared and take part in read, write and assignment statements. For example

```
C := 'A';

READ(D);

FOR C := '0' TO '9' DO WRITE(C);
```

The last of these examples relies on assertion (3) above. It may be clarified by considering each character to have a position number in the set of available characters. This position is likely not to be zero for '0', but it is one less than that for '1', etc.

Assuming C to be a character value and I to be an integer expression, two of the standard functions which may be used with characters are

ORD(C)   which yields the position or ordinal number of the character in the available set of characters

CHR(I)   which yields the character whose ordinal number is the value I

For example, given a number J less than 10, the ordinal value of the corresponding digit character is ORD('0') + J. Hence, the character corresponding to J is

```
CHR(ORD('0') + J)
```

When comparing character values (C and D say) it should be noted that if

```
ORD(C) < ORD(D)
```

that is, the character value D is further down the list of available characters than the character value C, then

```
C < D
```

Thus all of the comparison operators may be applied. For example

```
IF D <> 'X' THEN WRITE(D)

IF C > 'O' THEN (* STATEMENT *)
```

Example 4B is a complete program using character variables to read in arithmetic calculations and print the result.

Example 4B

```
(* PROGRAM TO ACT AS A HAND CALCULATOR *)
PROGRAM EX4B(INPUT,OUTPUT);
VAR OPERATOR      :CHAR;
    ANSWER,NEWNO :REAL;
BEGIN
ANSWER := 0; OPERATOR := '+';
REPEAT
    READ (NEWNO);
    CASE OPERATOR OF
     '+': ANSWER := ANSWER + NEWNO;
     '-': ANSWER := ANSWER - NEWNO;
     '*': ANSWER := ANSWER * NEWNO;
     '/': ANSWER := ANSWER / NEWNO
    END;
    READ (OPERATOR)
UNTIL OPERATOR = '=' ;
WRITELN ('ANSWER IS', ANSWER)
END.
```

4.6 The Basis of Decisions—Boolean

Boolean variables are declared in the **VAR** declaration as, for example

```
VAR P,Q : BOOLEAN;
```

They may only have one of the two values, TRUE or FALSE. Boolean values usually arise from the result of comparing expressions. For example, given an integer X

```
P := X < 4
```

gives P the value TRUE if X is less than 4 and FALSE if X is greater than or equal to 4.

Boolean expressions may be used wherever an expression is permitted, for example, on the right-hand side of assignment statements, in **CASE** and **FOR** statements, etc. In particular, the expression used in **IF**, **WHILE** and **UNTIL** statements must be a boolean expression.

A 'simple boolean expression' consists of a series of boolean values or bracketed 'boolean expressions', separated by **AND** and **OR** operators only. Each value or subexpression may be preceded by **NOT**. For example

```
P AND NOT(Q OR R) AND T
```

A simple expression of *any* of the types so far considered may be compared with a simple expression of the same type to form a 'boolean expression'. Note that this permits one comparison only, in each boolean expression (but see section 4.7). For example, the following are boolean expressions

```
P AND Q  =  R AND T

I + 4    =  J * K
```

The boolean operators are

NOT which has greater precedence than
AND which has greater precedence than
OR which has greater precedence than
= <> < > <= >= which all have equal precedence

where

NOT P	is TRUE if P is FALSE, otherwise it is FALSE
P AND Q	is TRUE if both P and Q are TRUE, otherwise it is FALSE
P OR Q	is TRUE if either or both of P and Q are TRUE, otherwise it is FALSE
P = Q	is TRUE if P and Q have the same boolean value, otherwise it is FALSE
P <> Q	is TRUE if P and Q have different boolean values, otherwise it is FALSE

The remaining operators are less often used when applied to boolean values. A text on boolean algebra [Gill, 1976] may be consulted, should their definition be of interest.

The words TRUE and FALSE may be used as boolean constants. However, their use is mostly limited to initialisation of boolean variables, since it is not normally necessary to use them in boolean expressions. For example, the correct statement

IF P THEN statement;

would only be made inefficient by substituting P = TRUE for P.

One standard function which may be used in boolean expressions is

ODD(X)   which yields the value TRUE if the integer
           expression X has an odd value, FALSE if it has an
           even value

Example 4C demonstrates how boolean variables may be used to store the
result of a comparison (of the first number against zero) for later use.

Example 4C

```
(* PRINT ALL NUMBERS WITH SAME SIGN AS FIRST.
   LAST NUMBER IS ZERO *)
PROGRAM EX4C(INPUT,OUTPUT);
VAR NUMBER    :REAL;
    FIRSTSIGN :BOOLEAN;
BEGIN
READ(NUMBER); WRITELN(NUMBER);
FIRSTSIGN := NUMBER>=0;
REPEAT
     READ(NUMBER);
     IF FIRSTSIGN = (NUMBER >= 0) THEN WRITELN(NUMBER)
UNTIL NUMBER = 0
END.
```

4.7 More Complex Conditions

It may be deduced from the previous section that a combination of comparisons
and boolean values may be used, wherever a boolean value is permitted. In particular, several conditions may be combined in the control statements **IF, UNTIL**
and **WHILE**. However, some care is required, since the comparison symbols
(=, <, etc.) are of lesser precedence than **OR, AND** and **NOT** and only one comparison operator may be used in each expression.

The complete set of operators discussed in this chapter has, in fact, the precedence relationship below. Here the higher operators are applied before the
lower.

highest **NOT**
         $*$ / **DIV MOD AND**   called the multiplying
                                 operators
         $+$ $-$ **OR**   called the adding operators
lowest $=$ $<$ $>$ $<>$ $<=$ $>=$ called the relational operators

Thus, for example

NOT A = B   means (**NOT** A) = B
A = B **AND** C   means A = (B **AND** C)
X = Y = Z   is   ILLEGAL

and the first two of these expressions only make sense if A, B and C are *boolean* variables. Where it is required to combine comparisons, brackets should be used. For example

```
IF (C >= '0') AND (C <= '9') THEN WRITE(C)

UNTIL (A = 0) OR (COUNT = 10)

WHILE (ERROR > 0.01) AND (I < 1000) DO

IF FIRSTSIGN = (NUMBER >= 0) THEN WRITELN(NUMBER)
```

The combination of boolean operators **OR**, **AND** and **NOT** is also of some interest. The precedence of these operators is such that

P OR Q AND NOT R

means

P OR (Q AND (NOT R))

Boolean expressions involving the **NOT** operator may often be simplified by making use of the facts

NOT (NOT A)   is the same as A
NOT (A AND B)   is the same as **(NOT A) OR (NOT B)**
NOT (A OR B)   is the same as **(NOT A) AND (NOT B)**
NOT (A = B)   is the same as A $<>$ B
and similarly for the other comparisons

Thus, for example

NOT $((A < B)$ AND $(C <> D))$

could be written as

$(A >= B)$ **OR** $(C = D)$

Cautionary Note

A boolean expression involving several simple boolean expressions may not always be fully evaluated on some computers. For example, in the following **WHILE** statement, if the value of A were 5, then some computers might not compare B with 2 because the result must be FALSE.

```
WHILE (A = 1) AND (B = 2) DO
    (* STATEMENT *)
```

This could affect the result of the program, if unevaluated parts of the boolean expression contained function calls (see chapter 6) or variables which do not have sensible values. It is safest to assume that boolean expressions *are* fully evaluated, but to take no advantage of this knowledge.

Exercises

4.1 Write the following algebraic expressions as Pascal simple arithmetic expressions

(a) $ax^2 + bx + c$ (b) $\frac{1}{2}(xy + \frac{z}{3x})$ (c) $\sqrt{(a^2 + b^2)}$

4.2 Write the following numbers in Pascal form such that the number before the decimal point is between 1 and 10.

(a) $1/10\,000\,000$ (b) $65\,526.0034$ (c) $\frac{-3}{4}$

4.3 Evaluate

(a)   2/3/4   (b)   2/2/4*5   (c)   2*3 **DIV** 4*5

(d)   23 **MOD** 4   (e)   ABS(ROUND(−4.7))

4.4 Write boolean expressions which are true if

(a)   I divides exactly by J

(b)   M is even

(c)   Y is neither in the range −2 to −1 nor the range +1 to +2

4.5 Simplify the following boolean expression
        NOT ((NOT P **OR** (X<Y)) **AND** (I=J))

Problem

Write a Pascal program to read in a line of characters terminating in a '.' symbol and to print out

(a)   the number of letters and
(b)   the number of digits and
(c)   the total number of characters.

5   An Introduction to Input and Output

5.1   READ and READLN

The Pascal statements to read data are best defined informally. As stated earlier, any number of data items may be read in one READ statement, by listing in brackets the variables to be assigned values. The declared type of each variable, in turn, determines the type of data item read—INTEGER, REAL or CHAR. Except for CHAR, all of the forms of non-named constant described in chapter 4 may appear as data. Items of non-character data must be separated from each other by at least one space or newline. Spaces and newlines are ignored before reading a non-character data item and the character which terminates the number is not read. Thus the following declarations and READ statements correspond to the data given

```
VAR   R, S : REAL;
      I, J : INTEGER;
      C, D : CHAR;

READ (C, D, R, I);
READ (J, S);
```

data

      AB   3.1   −16   15
                 −4.02E5

In the case of data to be read as characters, each character represents itself and spaces and the change to a newline *are* significant. Each space is read as a character. When the last character on a line has been read, the next character is not *immediately* available, and an attempt to read a character will yield a space. The change to the next line of data may be effected by the READLN statement, which ignores any remaining characters on the current line. In the same manner as READ, READLN may also specify data items to be read before skipping to the start of the next line of data. Example 5A illustrates the use of READLN; this ensures that the four characters are truly the first four on each line, since any spurious spaces or punctuation at the end of each line are ignored.

Example 5A

```
(* READ LINES OF 4 CHAR NAME AND NUMBER
   OUTPUT EACH LINE IN OTHER ORDER *)
PROGRAM EX5A(INPUT,OUTPUT);
VAR I,N,NUMBER :INTEGER;
    A,B,C,D    :CHAR;
BEGIN
READLN(N);
FOR I := 1 TO N DO
    BEGIN
    READ(A,B,C,D);
    READLN(NUMBER);
    WRITELN(NUMBER,A,B,C,D)
    END
END.
```

When reading characters, the act of reading a space is, of course, no guarantee
that the end of a line has been reached. Indeed, any number of spaces may
follow the last visible character on a line. This difficulty is overcome by use of
the boolean standard function EOLN. This is TRUE when all of the characters
on a line have been read, otherwise it is FALSE. For example, two characters,
possibly separated by a newline, may be read into the variables C and D by the
statements

```
READ (C);
IF EOLN THEN READLN;
READ(D)
```

5.2 WRITE and WRITELN

The basic form of the WRITE statement is the word WRITE followed by a
bracketed list of expressions. As with READ the type of each expression determines the type of item printed as a result. All four standard scalar types are
permitted, the word TRUE or FALSE being printed for a boolean expression.
In addition, a string of characters may be output, by enclosing them in ' symbols.
As with character constants, a ' itself must be given twice if it is included in a
string. As an exception to the general rule, it should be noted that a complete
integer expression is not acceptable as a REAL value to be printed. Such expressions should be assigned to a REAL variable, which may then be used in the
WRITE statement. Thus the following declarations, assignments and WRITE
statements might produce the output shown.

```
program:       .
               .
               VAR   R    : REAL;
                     I, J : INTEGER;
                     C    : CHAR;
                     B    : BOOLEAN;
               .
               .
               I := 3;
               J := 2;
               R := I/J;
               C := '*';
               B := I>J;
               WRITE ('IT''S PRINTED AS ', R, ' ', C);
               WRITE (I DIV J, B);
               .
               .
```

output:

IT'S PRINTED AS   1.5000000000000E+000 *   1   TRUE

Each item output is printed further to the right on the same line (see section 5.3 for how much further). The action taken when WRITE is used to print more than the width of the line permits, depends on the particular computer and the nature of the device used for printing. In order to enforce a change to a newline at a suitable point, WRITELN is used. The rules for WRITELN are identical to those of WRITE, except that the output device moves to the start of the next line, *after* printing any output specified. The following statements copy one line of input to the output, character by character. They illustrate the use of READLN, WRITELN and EOLN.

```
WHILE NOT EOLN DO
  BEGIN
  READ(C); WRITE(C)
  END;
READLN; WRITELN
```

If the output device used has sheets of paper, rather than a continuous roll, it may be sensible to divide output into separate pages. The change to a new page of output is normally automatic for the first page, but the standard procedure PAGE may be used as a statement to enforce subsequent changes to a new page. For example

```
IF LINECOUNT = 30 THEN PAGE †
```

† In some implementations, it is necessary to follow an identifier PAGE with a bracketed name. This is the name of a file giving the destination of the results. (See chapter 8.)

5.3   The Different Styles of Output

Where the aesthetics of output are of particular concern or where output is tabu-
lated, the exact number of characters output for each item must be controlled.
This may be done by following each such item in the WRITE statement, by one
or two positive integer values. For example

```
WRITE   (':', 'ANSWER IS' : 16, I+J : 4, C : 5);
WRITELN (R : 6 : 2)
```

These values may be specified as integer expressions.

The first value gives the minimum field width for the item. This is the minimum number of characters output. If the item requires less characters, it is preceded by a suitable number of spaces. If it requires more characters, as many as
needed are used. REAL items are always preceded by at least one space on output.

The second value following the WRITE item only applies to REAL values.
This gives the number of digits to be printed after the decimal point. If the
second value is given, the number is output in fixed-point notation. That is

   space sign integral part decimal point fractional part

If it is not given, only one decimal place is given before the decimal point and an
appropriate value follows the E symbol to give the true decimal magnitude. Thus
the statements above might output.

```
:          ANSWER IS  32    *  1.50
```

When tabulating results and outputting suitable captions above columns of
figures, it may be found useful to draw out a typical line of output on squared
paper. The exact spacing required may then easily be determined. For example,
an answer (no doubt improved) to the centigrade-to-Fahrenheit conversion program of chapter 2, could be program EX5B. This would be achieved by first
drawing

Example 5B

```
(* TABULATE CENTIGRADE INTEGER TEMPERATURES
   FROM 0 TO 99 DEGREES
   AGAINST THE FAHRENHEIT EQUIVALENT
   TO THE NEAREST 0.1 DEGREES *)
PROGRAM EX5B(OUTPUT);
CONST CONVERSION = 1.8;
      OFFSET = 32.0;
VAR CENTEMP  :INTEGER;
    FAHRTEMP :REAL;
BEGIN
WRITELN('CENTIGRADE FAHRENHEIT');
FOR CENTEMP := 0 TO 99 DO
     BEGIN
     FAHRTEMP := CENTEMP * CONVERSION + OFFSET;
     WRITELN(CENTEMP:2, ' ':7, FAHRTEMP:7:1)
     END
END.
```

The value of field width taken, if none is specified, depends on the particular computer used. However, typical values are

INTEGER	10
REAL	22 (including E, + or −, and 3 digits)
BOOLEAN	10
CHAR	1
STRING	length of the string

In addition, some computers may limit the length of line output (to, say, 136 characters) and/or use the first character of each line to control the output printer carriage. Where this is the case, the first character is not printed and the following meanings are given

+	no line feed (i.e. overprinting)
space	single spacing
0	double spacing
1	skip to top of next page before printing

Exercises

5.1 Write Pascal statements to read twenty lines of characters and output only the upper-case vowels.

5.2 Amend example 3L to output the results in a tabular style with headings at the top of the employee number and tax columns. In addition, output columns showing the data read for each employee.

Problem

Print the trigonometric values of sine, cosine, tangent, cosecant, secant and cotangent for values of angle of $0°$ to $45°$ in steps of $0.1°$. It would be sensible to put a $5°$ range on each page of output, with suitable headings at the top of each page. The following mathematical facts are true of the angle W

tangent W	$\equiv$	sine W/cosine W
cosecant W	$\equiv$	1/sine W (note sine $0° = 0$)
secant W	$\equiv$	1/cosine W
cotangent W	$\equiv$	1/tangent W (note tangent $0° = 0$)
π	$\equiv$	4 arctangent (1)
2π radians	$=$	$360°$

6 An Introduction to Procedures and Functions

6.1 Calling and Defining a Procedure

It may happen that a particular set of actions has to appear several times in a solution. We may avoid writing out the Pascal statements at every place they are required, by defining them to be a 'procedure'. A procedure gives a name to a set of actions, which may then be invoked or 'called' merely by referring to the name. This has the additional advantage of increased readability, of which more below and in chapter 13. A complete procedure is a declaration which must appear after the **VAR** declarations. Its form is as shown in figure 6.1. This is similar to the definition of a program given in chapter 2. A procedure may be considered as a program dedicated to some subtask of the problem, thus simplifying the over-all solution (see section 6.5 and chapter 13).

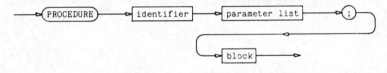

Figure 6.1

The top line of the syntax diagram describes the 'procedure heading'. The block or 'procedure body' consists of the declaration of identifiers to be used only in the procedure, followed by the Pascal statements required to perform the actions. Example 6A includes a declaration of a procedure called DRAWA-LINE and two calls for it. The purpose of the procedure is to draw a line on the output, above and below the result of the addition. This is achieved, on simple output devices, by outputting many − symbols.

Example 6A

```
(* ADD TWO NUMBERS AND PRINT NEATLY *)
PROGRAM EX6A(INPUT,OUTPUT);
VAR NUM1,NUM2,TOTAL : REAL;
PROCEDURE DRAWALINE;
    CONST LENGTH = 10;
    VAR I : INTEGER;
    BEGIN
    FOR I := 1 TO LENGTH DO
        WRITE('-');
    WRITELN
    END;
```

```
BEGIN
READ(NUM1, NUM2);
WRITELN(NUM1:10:3);
WRITELN(NUM2:10:3);
DRAWALINE;
TOTAL := NUM1 + NUM2;
WRITELN(TOTAL:10:3);
DRAWALINE
END.
```

With such a simple procedure, the program is not actually textually shorter than it would have been without the use of a procedure. However, it is easier to read, understand and modify. For example, suppose it was required to modify the program to draw the lines with alternate • and – symbols. However many calls of the procedure there are, only one change is needed—to the procedure body

```
PROCEDURE DRAWALINE;
    CONST LENGTH = 10;
    VAR I : INTEGER;
    BEGIN
    FOR I := 1 TO LENGTH DIV 2 DO
        WRITE('-.');
    IF ODD(LENGTH) THEN WRITE('-');
    WRITELN
    END;
```

Note that the program would now be as long and less readable if the procedure were not used!

6.2 Varying the Action—Value Parameters

The usefulness of a procedure is greatly enchanced if its action may be varied from one call to the next. This may be achieved by the use of 'parameters'. In their simplest form, these are variables used within the procedure, which are given a different starting value by each call. This kind of parameter is called a 'value parameter'. The types of all parameters are specified, within the round brackets, in the heading. Thus, if the DRAWALINE procedure were required to output a different length of line each time it was used, the quantity LENGTH could be made a parameter. Example 6B draws a histogram of suitable length lines, by reading in values and calling DRAWALINE with the nearest integer to each value. Negative values are drawn as a zero value and values over 100 are drawn as a line of length 100.

Example 6B

```
(* DRAW HISTOGRAM AS LINES OF APPROPRIATE LENGTH
    FOR VALUES READ *)
PROGRAM EX6B(INPUT,OUTPUT);
VAR X,Y,N  : INTEGER;
      NUMBER : REAL;
PROCEDURE DRAWALINE(LENGTH : INTEGER);
      VAR I : INTEGER;
      BEGIN
      FOR I := 1 TO LENGTH DO
            WRITE('-');
      WRITELN
      END;
BEGIN
READ(N);
FOR X := 1 TO N DO
      BEGIN
      READ(NUMBER);
      Y := ROUND(NUMBER);
      IF Y < 0 THEN
            DRAWALINE(0)
      ELSE IF Y > 100 THEN
                  DRAWALINE(100)
            ELSE DRAWALINE(Y)
      END
END.
```

The different values given for LENGTH–0, 100 and Y–are called 'actual parameters'. An actual value parameter may be any expression of the correct type. The name used in the heading and within the procedure, is called the 'formal parameter', since the procedure is formally written in terms of this name. Each formal value parameter (for example, LENGTH) is given the value of the corresponding actual parameter (for example, 100), before the procedure is entered.

6.3   Obtaining Results–Variable Parameters

The set of actions which form a self-contained procedure may produce results which are to be used later in the program. This is achieved by use of 'variable' parameters. In a procedure call, an actual parameter corresponding to a formal variable parameter must be given as a variable. Any list of formal variable parameters, in a procedure heading, is distinguished by preceding them with the delimiter **VAR**. A simplified syntax diagram of parameter list is given in figure 6.2.

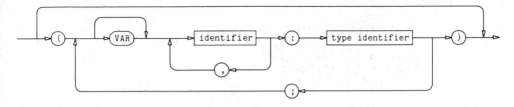

Figure 6.2

Thus, in example 6C, the actual variable parameters X and Y are changed in value by the SWAP procedure.

Example 6C

```
(* ORDER EACH OF N DATA PAIRS *)
PROGRAM EX6C(INPUT,OUTPUT);
VAR I,N : INTEGER;
    X,Y : REAL;
PROCEDURE SWAP(VAR P,Q : REAL);
     VAR TEMP : REAL;
     BEGIN
     TEMP := P;
     P    := Q;
     Q    := TEMP
     END;
BEGIN
READ(N);
FOR I := 1 TO N DO
     BEGIN
     READ(X,Y);
     IF X > Y THEN SWAP(X,Y);
     WRITELN(X,Y)
     END;
WRITELN('ARE THE ORDERED PAIRS')
END.
```

Within a procedure, any operation on a formal variable parameter (for example, P and Q) is, in fact, performed on the corresponding actual parameter (for example, X and Y). Hence, in example 6C, the values of X and Y are swapped over by the procedure call. Contrarily, formal *value* parameters may be changed in value, without affecting any variables outside the procedure.

The procedure of example 6D shows how both value and variable parameters may be used in the same procedure. At the procedure call, the one *value* parameter INS is given the value read in previously. The operations within the procedure on the four formal *variable* parameters—M, Y, F and I—are actually applied to A, B, C and D, which are then printed. Note that, where a procedure has several variable parameters, the actual parameters should be *distinct* variables.

Example 6D

```
(* CONVERT A NUMBER OF INCHES
   INTO MILES, YARDS, FEET AND INCHES *)
PROGRAM EX6D(INPUT,OUTPUT);
VAR A,B,C,D,NUMBER : INTEGER;
PROCEDURE CONVERT (VAR M,Y,F,I : INTEGER;
                        INS : INTEGER);
        BEGIN
        M := INS DIV (1760*36);
        INS := INS MOD (1760*36);
        Y := INS DIV 36;
        INS := INS MOD 36;
        F := INS DIV 12;
        I := INS MOD 12
        END;
BEGIN
READ(NUMBER);
CONVERT(A,B,C,D,NUMBER);
WRITELN(A:4, ' MILES,',
        B:4, ' YARDS,',
        C:1, ' FEET AND',
        D:2, ' INCHES')
END.
```

6.4   Calculating One Value—Functions

A procedure is used to identify a set of actions. A 'function' identifies a calculation or expression by associating a name and parameters with the calculation of a value. The name of the function and a bracketed list of actual parameters may be used wherever a value might be used. For example

```
Y := MAX(P,Q) + 1
```

specifies that a function MAX is to be called with actual parameters P and Q, and that resulting value plus one is to be assigned to Y. As with any other value, the type of value calculated by the function must be consistent with the expression in which it is used. The type † of the function is specified in the heading of its declaration, which is similar in form to a procedure declaration (see figure 6.3).

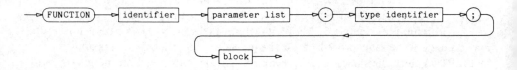

Figure 6.3

†The type may not be a structured type (see chapter 7).

The body of a function declaration is a block and may contain any set of statements. However, an assignment to the name of the function must be included. Obeying this statement defines the value of the function. Thus the declaration of the MAX function might be

```
FUNCTION MAX(X,Y : REAL) : REAL;
    BEGIN
    IF X > Y THEN
        MAX := X
    ELSE MAX := Y
    END
```

This declares a function called MAX which has two REAL value parameters and calculates a REAL value. Functions which use variable parameters may be calculating several results and hence would be better expressed as a procedure.

A complete program using both a procedure and a function is given in example 6E. Two lengths given in non-metric units are added by making use of a function which calculates the equivalent value in inches. This program also illustrates a useful feature of procedures and functions—that they may easily be reused in another program.

Example 6E

```
(* LENGTHS ARITHMETIC *)
PROGRAM EX6E(INPUT,OUTPUT);
VAR A,B,C,D,TOTAL : INTEGER;
PROCEDURE CONVERT (VAR M,Y,F,I : INTEGER;
                       INS : INTEGER);
    BEGIN
    M := INS DIV (1760*36);
    INS := INS MOD (1760*36);
    Y := INS DIV 36;
    INS := INS MOD 36;
    F := INS DIV 12;
    I := INS MOD 12
    END;
FUNCTION INCHES(M,Y,F,I : INTEGER) : INTEGER;
    BEGIN
    INCHES := (((M*1760) + Y)*3 + F)*12 + I
    END;
BEGIN
READ(A,B,C,D);
TOTAL := INCHES(A,B,C,D);
READ(A,B,C,D);
TOTAL := TOTAL + INCHES(A,B,C,D);
CONVERT(A,B,C,D,TOTAL);
WRITELN('SUM IS', TOTAL, ' INCHES - I.E.');
WRITELN(A:4, ' MILES,',
        B:4, ' YARDS,',
        C:1, ' FEET AND',
        D:2, ' INCHES')
END.
```

6.5 The Scope of Identifiers

Example 6F calculates the sum of a series of values, where each value is taken as the average of a set of numbers given on one line of data. Many physical measurements are taken this way, for example, total yearly sunshine as a sum of daily average readings.

Example 6F

```
            (* PRINT SUM OF N VALUES.
               EACH VALUE IS AVERAGE OF SET OF NUMBERS *)
            PROGRAM EX6F(INPUT,OUTPUT);
            CONST WIDTH=10;
            VAR I,N,COUNT          : INTEGER;
(*L6*)          LINEAVERAGE,TOTAL : REAL;
            PROCEDURE DRAWALINE;
                VAR I : INTEGER;
                BEGIN
                FOR I := 1 TO WIDTH DO
                    WRITE('-');
                WRITELN
                END;
            FUNCTION AVERAGE(READCOUNT : INTEGER) : REAL;
                VAR I         : INTEGER;
(*L16*)             TOTAL,NUM : REAL;
                BEGIN
(*L18*)         TOTAL := 0;
                FOR I := 1 TO READCOUNT DO
                    BEGIN
                    READ(NUM);
(*L22*)             TOTAL := TOTAL + NUM
                    END;
                AVERAGE := TOTAL / READCOUNT
                END;
            BEGIN
(*L27*)     TOTAL := 0; READ(N);
            FOR I := 1 TO N DO
                BEGIN
                READ(COUNT);
                LINEAVERAGE := AVERAGE(COUNT);
                WRITELN(LINEAVERAGE : WIDTH : 2);
(*L33*)         TOTAL := TOTAL + LINEAVERAGE
                END;
            DRAWALINE;
(*L36*)     WRITELN(TOTAL : WIDTH : 2);
            DRAWALINE
            END.
```

A point of interest in this example is which TOTAL is referred to on lines 18, 22, 27, 33 and 36—the TOTAL declared on line 6 or line 16? The validity of the use of the constant WIDTH and variable I also requires some scrutiny. These doubts are resolved by defining the 'scope' of identifiers, meaning the area of a program for which the declaration of an identifier is valid. The scope of an identifier is the block (program, procedure or function) in which it is defined and any enclosed block which does not re-define it. In addition (with one exception—see chapter 14), every identifier must be declared before it is used. Reducing example 6F to a skeleton of declarations only, figure 6.4 demonstrates the scope of all the identifiers.

Skeleton Program EX6F	*Identifiers which may be used*
| ```
CONST WIDTH = 10;
VAR I,N,COUNT        : INTEGER;
    LINEAVERAGE,TOTAL : REAL;
PROCEDURE DRAWALINE;
        VAR I : INTEGER;
        BEGIN

        END;
FUNCTION AVERAGE
        (READCOUNT : INTEGER) : REAL;
        VAR I        : INTEGER;
            TOTAL,NUM : REAL;
        BEGIN

        END;
BEGIN

END.
``` | ```

I                    ⊐ of DRAWALINE
DRAWALINE †          ⌐
WIDTH, N, COUNT,     │ of PROGRAM
LINEAVERAGE, TOTAL   ⌐

READCOUNT, I,        ⌐
TOTAL, NUM           ⌐ of AVERAGE
DRAWALINE, AVERAGE ⌐
WIDTH, N, COUNT    † │ of PROGRAM
LINEAVERAGE        ⌐

WIDTH, I, N, COUNT, ⌐
LINEAVERAGE, TOTAL, │ of PROGRAM
DRAWALINE, AVERAGE  ⌐
``` |

Figure 6.4 Skeleton program EX6F showing scope of identifiers (†See chapter 13 for use of procedures/functions within other procedures/functions)

Thus it may be seen that the two variables called TOTAL and three variables called I have scopes which give a sensible meaning to the program.

A use of an identifier in the same block as its declaration is called a 'local' reference. A use of an identifier declared in an outer block is called a 'non-local' reference. Thus use of the constant WIDTH in DRAWALINE is a *valid* non-local reference. Non-local reference is useful for constants, procedures and type definitions (see chaper 7), but should be avoided in the case of scalar variables. A non-local variable reference is often better expressed as an additional parameter to the procedure (see chapter 13).

The formal parameters given in a procedure heading and any label numbers declared in the LABEL declaration have the same scope as identifiers declared within the procedure.

Exercises

6.1 Alter program EX6A to output a line of + symbols between the first two numbers printed. This will require an additional parameter to the procedure.

6.2 Many programs may be suitably incorporated into larger programs by rewriting them as a procedure or function, with suitable parameters. Rewrite the programs EX3A to EX3C as procedures/functions. It may be necessary to change the WRITELN statements into function result assignments.

6.3 Draw boxes round the program, procedure and function of example 6E and demonstrate the scope of all of the identifiers.

Problems

6.1 Write a function MIN which gives the minimum of two numbers as its result. Use this and the MAX function in a program which will print the maximum, minimum and average values of a set of numbers read.

6.2 Write a program to perform addition of 'times' given in years, weeks, days and hours. The solution should include a procedure and a function and it may be assumed that there are exactly 365 days in a year.

7 Data Types

7.1 The Concept of Type

This chapter contains a complete and formal discussion of the concept of type. This concept has its origins in mathematics and logical reasoning. It was introduced to help to remove ambiguities and to identify meaningless statements. In a programming language the concept of type allows the programmer to structure the data in terms of the problem to be solved rather than the computer to be used. In the context of Pascal it has several important consequences as follows.

(1) Every item in Pascal, whether it is a constant, a variable, a function or an expression, is of one and only one type. The type of a variable determines a set of values, one of which may be assumed by the variable at any time.
(2) The type of an item may always be deduced by an examination of the program text. It is not necessary to execute the program to discover the type of an item.
(3) For each type a limited set of operations is defined, which may be applied to values of the type. The programmer may extend this set of operations by defining procedures and functions.
(4) The use of data types introduces a redundancy into the language, which helps in the detection of errors.

The number of distinct values belonging to a type is called the 'cardinality' of the type. So, for example, the cardinality of the type boolean is two.

Most of the operations provided in Pascal are limited in the types of value to which they may be applied. There are, however, two operations which can be sensibly applied to the members of any data type. These are

(1) assignment, and
(2) tests for equality and inequality.

For practical reasons, these operations are not provided in Pascal for all types. The availability or otherwise of these operations will be dealt with later.

7.2 Type Definitions

In mathematics, different alphabets and founts are normally used to identify the different types. This is not possible with a programming language because most computers will only accept a limited number of different characters. As a consequence, every variable and function must have its type declared using variable and function declarations.

It is also possible, indeed it is normal, to declare the types created in a program using type definitions. In some cases, however, it will be simpler explicitly to define the type in the variable declaration. The form of a type definition is shown in figure 7.1.

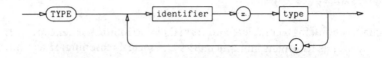

Figure 7.1

A complete syntax diagram for 'type' will be found in appendix I, but individual parts of the diagram will be given at suitable points in the text. *Note*: There are four places in the syntax of Pascal where a type identifier *must* be used

(1) formal parameter section (see chapter 6)
(2) function result type (see chapter 6)
(3) tagfield type specification (see chapter 12)
(4) pointer type specification (see chapter 14).

7.3 Unstructured Data Types

In Pascal all the unstructured data types are 'scalar' types. A scalar type has the following characteristics.

(1) The values may not be subdivided to expose values of another type.
(2) The values are distinct from each other and from the values of any other type.
(3) The values are ordered.
(4) The assignment operation is defined.
(5) All the relational operators are defined.
(6) With the exception of the type real, a member of any scalar type may be used as
    (a) the parameter of the standard functions ORD, PRED and SUCC,
    (b) the selector in a **CASE** statement, or
    (c) the control variable in a **FOR** statement.

Scalar types in Pascal are either standard or user-defined.

SUCC and PRED

Since the scalar types are ordered, all but the extreme values in the type will have a predecessor and a successor.

PRED(X) yields the predecessor of X, if one exists
SUCC(X) yields the successor to X, if one exists

These functions are rarely used for integers because

$$SUCC(I) \equiv I + 1$$
$$PRED(I) \equiv I - 1$$

7.3.1   User-defined Scalar Types

7.3.1.1   Scalar Enumeration Types

The simplest way of defining a new type is by specifying, in order, all of its
values. The values of the new type will be represented by identifiers, which
will be the constants of the new type. The form of such a specification is shown
in figure 7.2.

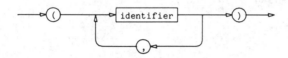

Figure 7.2

Examples

```
TYPE SUIT           = (CLUB,DIAMOND,HEART,SPADE);
     DAY            = (SAT,SUN,MON,TUE,WED,THU,FRI);
     PRIMARYCOLOUR  = (RED,YELLOW,BLUE);
     FLOOR          = (GROUND,LOWERFIRST,FIRST,SECOND);
VAR  PAYDAY,DAYOFF  : DAY;
     TRUMP          : SUIT;
     PAINT          : PRIMARYCOLOUR;
     COATS          : INTEGER;
     UNDERCOAT      : BOOLEAN;


CASE PAINT OF
   RED    : BEGIN
              COATS := 1; UNDERCOAT := FALSE
            END;
   YELLOW : BEGIN
              COATS := 2; UNDERCOAT := TRUE
            END;
   BLUE   : BEGIN
              COATS := 2; UNDERCOAT := FALSE
            END
END;
DAYOFF := SUCC(PAYDAY);
TRUMP := SPADE;
```

Notes: (a) The functions SUCC and PRED are only defined if a successor or predecessor value exists. So

```
PAINT := SUCC(BLUE);
```

is ridiculous.

(b) The ordinal value of the first constant of an enumerated type is 0. Consequently ORD (BLUE) yields 2.

(c) The ordering specified by the definition is such that, for example

DIAMOND < HEART

is true.

(d) The type boolean behaves as if BOOLEAN = (FALSE, TRUE).

If enumerated types were not provided it would be necessary to resort to the following

```
CONST RED = 0; YELLOW = 1; BLUE = 2;
VAR   PAINT : INTEGER;
```

this will, of course, permit

```
PAINT := RED;
```

but it also allows ridiculous statements, such as

```
PAINT := ORD('W'); PAINT := 4;
```

7.3.1.2 Subrange Types

In many circumstances when a variable is declared to be of a certain scalar type, it is known that it will only be used to hold a subset of the values of the type. This is almost always true of integer variables.

For any scalar type (except real), it is possible to create a new type whose values are a subrange of the values of the original type. The latter is referred to as the associated scalar type. A subrange type retains all the properties of the associated scalar type with a restriction on the range of its values.

It is the associated scalar type which is used to determine the legality, or otherwise, of the use of subrange variables and functions. However, although assignment to a subrange variable is legal, it may cause an error when executed, if the value to be assigned exceeds the declared subrange.

Subrange types have several advantages.

(1) The readability of programs is improved.
(2) The reduction in cardinality may save storage space.
(3) Run time checks may be included automatically in a program to verify the subrange declarations, by checking all assignments to subrange variables. This will help to find errors in a program.
(4) The cost of other diagnostic run time checks may be significantly decreased.

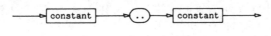

Figure 7.3

The form of a subrange specification is shown in figure 7.3.

The first constant specifies the lower bound of the range and the second constant specifies the upper bound. There must be at least one value in the range. The type of the constants determines the associated scalar type.

Examples

```
TYPE WEEKEND     = SAT..SUN;
     UPPERFLOOR  = LOWERFIRST..SECOND;
     LETTER      = 'A'..'Z'; (* BUT SEE 7.3.2 *)
     MONTHLENGTH = 28..31;
```

7.3.2 The Standard Scalar Types

The standard scalar types and the operations provided for them have been described in earlier chapters. For some of the standard scalar types, there are a few details relating to the concept of type which have not yet been described.

Integer In mathematics there is an infinite number of whole numbers. The type integer in Pascal is, in fact, a subrange of the integers. The subrange is

$$-\text{MAXINT} .. \text{MAXINT}$$

where MAXINT is an implementation-dependent constant. On implementations known to the authors, MAXINT varies from 32767 to 281474976710655. The integer operations are defined, if and only if the operands and the result are in this subrange. The results of all such operations are exact.

As a consequence of these restrictions, the associative and distributive laws of arithmetic do not always apply.

Real In mathematics the reals are an infinite, continuous set of values. In a computer the reals are represented by a finite set of values; each one of these representative real values represents an interval in the continuum of real values. The values are usually stored as a mantissa and an exponent. For example, 125.3 might have a mantissa of 1.253 and an exponent of 2. In computing parlance this is floating-point representation; to the owners of pocket calculators it is scientific representation.

The choice of such a representation has several consequences.

(1) There are some very large and very small values which cannot be represented.

Attempts to produce such values will usually produce an error action which is dependent on the computer system being used.

(2) Each real number will have, approximately, the same number of significant figures in its representation. As a consequence of this, the error in very large real numbers will be large in absolute terms.

(3) The representative real values are not evenly distributed across the range of values. There are approximately as many representative real values between 0.1 and 1 as between 100000 and 1000000.

Since the representation of real values is inexact, the arithmetic performed on them is also inexact. In particular, the normal algebraic laws of association, etc., do not in general apply. The development of methods to solve problems on a computer, despite these difficulties, is a subject called numerical mathematics. There are, however, a few simple rules.

(1) Real values should never be tested for equality.
(2) Care must be exercised when converting real values into integers.
(3) Avoid calculations which may subtract almost equal values, since this can produce errors due to the loss of many significant digits.

Char   The type CHAR denotes a finite, ordered set of characters. Whether a particular character is a member of this set, and its ordinal value if it is, are both implementation dependent. Hence the ordering of the characters is implementation dependent. There are two properties which must hold for all Pascal implementations

(1) the decimal digits are ordered and contiguous, that is

$$\text{SUCC ('0')} = \text{'1'}, \text{SUCC ('1')} = \text{'2'}, \text{etc.}$$

(2) the letters are ordered, that is

$$\text{'A'} < \text{'B'} < \text{'C'} \ldots < \text{'Y'} < \text{'Z'}$$

but are not necessarily contiguous.

For convenience in this book, tests to ascertain whether a character value is alphabetic or not will assume that all the values between 'A' and 'Z' represent letters.

7.4   Structured Data Types

A structured data type is defined in terms of one or more previously defined data types, using a structuring method. These types are called the 'constituent' types. A value of a structured type is made up of components, which are values of its constituent types. If there is only one constituent type, the term 'base' type is used. There are two operations which are specific to structured types.

These are selection and construction. A 'selector' takes a variable of a structured type and yields as its result a component of the structure. A 'constructor' is used to generate a structured value from its component values.

Pascal provides five distinct structuring methods which will be the subject of chapters 8 to 12. Where necessary, some restrictions have been placed on the use of these structuring methods to ensure that they may be efficiently realised. The structured types resulting from the application of these structuring methods are of two kinds, namely elementary and advanced.

An elementary data type has a finite cardinality. An advanced data type has an infinite cardinality.

7.5 Data Representation

In general, the Pascal programmer need only be concerned with data types in the abstract, since all the structuring methods of Pascal can be efficiently implemented. Very often, however, the need for an efficient selection operation results in a variable of a structured type occupying more storage space than its cardinality suggests is necessary. If storage space is at a premium, a packed structured type may be appropriate.

The definition of any structuring method may be preceded by the prefix **PACKED**. This is a request by the programmer for a reduction in the storage space needed by this structured type, even if the result is a less efficient selection operation. The extent to which this request is honoured is implementation dependent.

The systematic introduction of the prefix **PACKED** *has no effect on the meaning of a program* with one minor exception, namely that components of packed structures may not be used as actual *variable* parameters.

7.6 Type Compatibility

In many instances in a Pascal program, the legality of the program relies on the use of items of identical or at least compatible types.

Scalar Types The type of a constant, whether it be integer, real, boolean, char or enumerated scalar, is self-evident.

The type of a variable or function is given by its declaration.

The type of an expression may be deduced from the types of the operands and the result types of the operators.

The validity of all operations involving subrange variables is determined by their associated scalar types.

Whenever a real value is required and an integer value is not permitted, an integer value may be used but it will be converted automatically into a real value.

Structured Types   Operations involving variables of structured types require that their types are identical. The following simple rules will guarantee that two items are of identical type. Their types are identical if either

(1) they were declared in the same variable declaration, or
(2) they were declared using the same type identifier, which has not been redefined.

Additional rules relating to string constants and set constructors will be given in later chapters.

Exercises

7.1 Find out the cardinality of the types integer and char provided by the Pascal system that you use.

7.2 Find out the precision and range of values which the type real provides.

7.3 Examine the example programs from the earlier chapters to see whether there were any opportunities for using enumerated scalar or subrange types.

8 An Advanced Data Type— the Sequential File

8.1 The Concept of a Sequence

The easiest way to explain the concept of a sequence is by using an example. Given a set S whose elements are A and B, the following are all sequences of the elements of S

A, B, ABA, BBB, ABAB, etc.

In addition to these obvious sequences, it is possible to have a sequence which contains no As and no Bs. This is the empty sequence. Using the empty sequence as a starting point, all sequences of the elements of S can be seen to be either

(1) the empty sequence, or
(2) a sequence of the elements of S followed by an element of S.

The sequence A is the empty sequence followed by A. The sequence ABAB is the sequence ABA followed by B, etc.

A consequence of this definition is that, although every sequence is itself of finite length, the number of possible sequences is infinite.

The sequence occurs as a wide variety of data structures in programming, for example, stacks, queues, character strings, sequential files, etc. These data structures are so different in character that it is not possible to provide a single sequence data type efficiently. Instead, Pascal provides dynamic variables which permit the programmer to implement advanced structured types tailored to the specific application. There is, however, one form of the sequence which is so fundamental (it forms the basis of all input/output in Pascal) that it is explicitly provided. This is the sequential file.

8.2 The Sequential File

A sequential file is a sequence with two distinct modes of operation. A file may be examined (but not altered) one element at a time, starting at the beginning. A file may be created (but not examined) by appending new components to the end of an originally empty file. In both cases the files must be processed sequentially. Since only one component of a file is accessible at any time, only the current component needs to be held in the main computer store. The file itself is usually held on the backing store of the computer. Not surprisingly, neither the assignment operation nor the equality relation is available for file types or for any type with a file component.

8.2.1 File Definitions

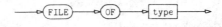

Figure 8.1

The form of a file specification is shown in figure 8.1.

Examples

```
TYPE TEXT          = FILE OF CHAR;
     BINGOPLAYERS = FILE OF BINGOCARD;
     INTFILE       = FILE OF INTEGER;
```

Notes: (a) Although the file specification part may incorporate any of the possible 'type' alternatives, a type identifier is most commonly used.
(b) The base type of a file may be any type, but files of files are rarely implemented.
(c) The type TEXT = **FILE OF** CHAR is standard.

8.2.2 File Creation

In this section and the next the following declarations are assumed

```
VAR  ITEM : X;
     F    : FILE OF X;
     CH   : CHAR;
```

The process of file creation is initiated by calling the standard procedure REWRITE, thus

```
REWRITE(F)
```

This discards the sequence currently associated with F and sets F to the empty file.

Associated with the file F there is a 'buffer variable', denoted by F↑. This represents the current component of the file. A new component is added to the end of the file by assigning it to the buffer variable and calling the standard procedure PUT, thus

```
F↑ := ITEM;  PUT(F)
```

This pair of statements occurs so frequently that the two statements have been made into the standard procedure WRITE.

```
WRITE(F, ITEM)
```

is equivalent to

```
F↑ := ITEM;  PUT(F)
```

The process of creating may be summarised by the following general scheme

```
REWRITE(F);
WHILE GENERATIONISTOCONTINUE DO
  BEGIN
  GENERATE(ITEM); WRITE(F,ITEM)
  END;
```

Notes: (a) When the procedure PUT appends the contents of the buffer variable to the file, it leaves the value of the buffer variable undefined.
(b) If the file parameter of WRITE is omitted then the file OUTPUT is assumed. So WRITE(CH) is the same as WRITE(OUTPUT, CH). This also applies to the WRITELN and PAGE procedures described in chapter 5.
(c) The second parameter of the WRITE procedure must be of a type compatible with the base type of the file, that is, the expanded form of the WRITE procedure must result in a legal assignment statement. The only exceptions to this, which occur for text files, have been described in chapter 5.
(d) The procedure REWRITE may not be applied to the file OUTPUT.

8.2.3   File Examination

The process of file scanning (or reading) is initiated by calling the standard procedure RESET, thus

```
RESET(F)
```

This sets the buffer variable to the first component of the file F unless the file is empty. If the file is empty, the value of the buffer variable is undefined and the condition 'end of file' becomes true. The standard function EOF may be used to determine whether the end of the file has been reached. The standard procedure GET is used to advance the buffer variable to the next component in the file. Again, if there is no next component, the buffer variable is undefined and the end of file condition becomes true. The process of file examination may be summarised by the following scheme

```
RESET(F);
WHILE NOT EOF(F) DO
  BEGIN
  READ(F,ITEM); PROCESS(ITEM)
  END;
```

Notes: (a) READ(F, ITEM) is equivalent to ITEM := F↑; GET(F). The type of the second parameter of READ must be compatible with the base type of the file. The only exceptions to this, which occur for textfiles, have been described in chapter 5.

(b) The file parameter may be omitted from both READ and EOF, in which case the file INPUT is assumed, that is, EOF(INPUT) is the same as EOF. This also applies to READLN and EOLN, which were described in chapter 5.
(c) The procedures READ and GET may not be called if the end of file condition is true.
(d) The procedure RESET may not be applied to the file INPUT.

8.3   Internal and External Files

Files which are used for input (or output) by a Pascal program will exist before (or after) the program is executed. These files are external to the program and are called 'external' files. Every external file must be specified in the program heading, for example

```
PROGRAM EX8A(INPUT,OUTPUT,OLDFILE,NEWFILE);
```

Also, every external file (except INPUT and OUTPUT) must be declared as a variable in the main program. The files INPUT and OUTPUT are automatically declared as textfiles if they occur in the program heading.

Files which are not used for input or output are used for purposes internal to the program. These are called 'internal' files. Internal files are simply local variables.
Notes: (a) It is perfectly legal to have program headings which include neither INPUT nor OUTPUT, but implementation restrictions to the contrary are quite common.
(b) When execution of a Pascal program starts, the operations of RESET(INPUT) and REWRITE(OUTPUT) are implied if the files occur in the program heading.
(c) The program parameters specified in the program heading are usually but not necessarily files.

8.4   Textfiles

Textfiles are unlike all other file types in that they are not simply sequences of values of some type. Textfiles are internally structured into lines using end of line markers which are not values of the type char. So textfiles may either be treated as sequences of characters (the end of line markers are then interpreted as spaces) or as a sequence of lines of characters. As a consequence two quite different schemes may be applied to the processing of textfiles. In the first case the file schemes which have already been described are suitable. If textfiles are to be processed as sequences of lines then a more complex scheme is necessary.

Writing a sequence of lines

```
REWRITE(F);
WHILE GENERATIONISTOCONTINUE DO
  BEGIN
  WHILE THELINEISINCOMPLETE DO
    BEGIN
    GENERATE(CH); WRITE(F,CH)
    END;
  WRITELN(F)
  END;
```

Reading a sequence of lines

```
RESET(F);
WHILE NOT EOF(F) DO
  BEGIN
  WHILE NOT EOLN(F) DO
    BEGIN
    READ(F,CH); PROCESS(CH)
    END;
  LINEENDPROCESS;
  READLN(F)
  END;
```

None of the schemes described so far is applicable to the problem of processing numbers composed of characters. There is a small difficulty in this area. As has been explained in chapter 5, the READ procedure will accept character representations of numbers, skipping over any leading spaces and end of line markers. The READ procedure does not skip over trailing spaces. This means that the end of file condition will *not* become true after the last number has been read if there are any trailing spaces or end of line markers. This rather annoying little difficulty has several possible solutions

(1) terminate the number sequence with a special character
(2) arrange the numbers into a sequence of lines of numbers
(3) include statements to skip the trailing spaces after a number.

A Note on End of Line Markers

When the end of line marker was introduced in chapter 5, the procedure GET and the buffer variable had not been described.

The end of line condition is true when the buffer variable contains the space character resulting from *getting* the end of line marker. This occurs when the last character on the line has been *read*. An exact description of the READLN procedure is

```
READLN(F)
```

is equivalent to

```
WHILE NOT EOLN(F) DO GET(F);
GET(F)
```

8.5   A Simple Text Editor

The problem is to write a text editor which edits files a line at a time. It will
interpret four simple commands. Each command appears on a separate line.
The commands are

```
C  n    copy up to but not including line number n
S  n    skip up to but not including line number n
I  n    insert n lines of text from the command file
E       copy the rest of the old file to the new file and end
        the edit
```

where n is any positive integer. These commands can only be sensibly written
in order of increasing line numbers. So the editor needs to scan the command
file and the old file once, producing a new file at the same time. The over-all
scheme for the editor is

```
PROGRAM EX8A(INPUT,OUTPUT,OLDFILE,NEWFILE);
VAR OLDFILE,NEWFILE : TEXT;
BEGIN (* MAIN PROGRAM *)
(* INITIALISE *)
REPEAT
  (* READ COMMAND *)
  (* OBEY COMMAND *)
UNTIL (CH = 'E') OR ERROR;
IF ERROR THEN WRITELN(' ERROR IN EDIT ')
END.
```

The READ COMMAND part is straightforward. The OBEY COMMAND
part can be refined to be

```
IF (* VALID COMMAND *) THEN
  CASE CH OF
    'C' : (* PERFORM COPY COMMAND *)
    'S' : (* PERFORM SKIP COMMAND *)
    'I' : (* PERFORM INSERT COMMAND *)
    'E' : (* PERFORM END COMMAND *)
  END
ELSE ERROR := TRUE;
```

The COPY, INSERT and END operations all involve the copying of one or
more lines of text from one file to another. This suggests that a procedure should
be written to perform the task. This procedure is simply the inner loop of the
scheme for processing files of lines of characters. The operation of skipping a
line can be simply achieved by READLN(OLDFILE).

The complete program is as follows.

```
PROGRAM EX8A(INPUT,OUTPUT,OLDFILE,NEWFILE);
VAR OLDFILE,NEWFILE : TEXT;
    CH               : CHAR;
    N,I,CURRENTLINE : 1..MAXINT;
    ERROR : BOOLEAN;
PROCEDURE COPYLINE(VAR F1,F2 : TEXT);
   VAR CH : CHAR;
   BEGIN
   WHILE NOT EOLN(F1) DO
     BEGIN
     READ(F1,CH); WRITE(F2,CH)
     END;
   READLN(F1); WRITELN(F2)
   END; (* COPYLINE *)
BEGIN (* MAIN PROGRAM *)
(* INITIALISE *)
RESET(OLDFILE); REWRITE(NEWFILE);
CURRENTLINE := 1; ERROR := FALSE;
REPEAT
  (* READ COMMAND *)
  READ(CH);
  IF CH <> 'E' THEN READ(N);
  READLN;
  (* OBEY COMMAND *)
  IF (CH='E') OR (CH='C') OR (CH='S') OR (CH='I') THEN
    CASE CH OF
      'C' : (* PERFORM COPY COMMAND *)
              BEGIN
              ERROR := N < CURRENTLINE;
              FOR I := 1 TO N - CURRENTLINE DO
                COPYLINE(OLDFILE,NEWFILE);
              CURRENTLINE := N
              END;
      'S' : (* PERFORM SKIP COMMAND *)
              BEGIN
              ERROR := N < CURRENTLINE;
              FOR I := 1 TO N - CURRENTLINE DO
                READLN(OLDFILE);
              CURRENTLINE := N
              END;
      'I' : (* PERFORM INSERT COMMAND *)
              FOR I := 1 TO N DO
                COPYLINE(INPUT,NEWFILE);
      'E' : (* PERFORM END COMMAND *)
              WHILE NOT EOF(OLDFILE) DO
                COPYLINE(OLDFILE,NEWFILE)
    END
  ELSE ERROR := TRUE
UNTIL (CH = 'E') OR ERROR;
IF ERROR THEN WRITELN(' ERROR IN EDIT ')
END.
```

Exercises

8.1 Write a program to calculate the number of end of line markers in a text file.

8.2 Write a program to compute average, maximum and minimum line length of a text file. End of line markers must not be counted as characters.

8.3 Write a program to merge two ordered files of INTEGER to produce a single ordered file.

8.4 Write a statement which will skip characters on the file INPUT until a letter has to be read.

8.5 As exercise 8.4, except that the skipping stops before the letter is read.

Problem

Write a program which will convert several amounts of money expressed in one currency to equivalent amounts in another currency. In addition, these amounts of money should be expressed in terms of the minimum number of notes and coins needed in the new currency to form the required sum. Print out the numbers of each denomination required.

Data for the program will consist of

(1) On a textual input file
    (a) the conversion rate
    (b) several sums of money to be converted.
(2) On a **FILE OF** REAL in descending order by value, the denominations of each coin and note in the new currency.

Note: You should check that the converted sum of money is equal to the sum of all the coins and notes which are used to represent it.

9 Elementary Structured Types 1—the Set

9.1 An Introduction to Set Theory

The theory of sets is a branch of mathematics which was originated by Cantor
in the late nineteenth century. Although a detailed examination of set theory
would be out of place in a text on programming, a brief introduction to set
theory is necessary for an understanding of sets in Pascal.

A set is any collection of objects which are to be conceived of as a whole.
The objects within a set are known as the members or the elements of that set.
Some examples of sets are

> the prime numbers whose magnitude is less than 50
> all computer science students
> all students able to program in Pascal
> all students able to program in Fortran
> the buttons in an automatic lift (elevator).

It is the basis of set theory that a set is defined by its members. Consequently,
two sets are the same if and only if their members are the same. There is no
ordering involved here, so the following sets are all the same

$$\{1, 3, 5\} \quad \{5, 3, 1\} \quad \text{and} \quad \{3, 5, 1\} \quad \text{etc.}$$

If all the members of one set are also members of another set, then the first
set is said to be 'included' in the second. So, for example, $\{1, 5\}$ is included in
$\{1, 3, 5\}$. Since these two sets are unequal, the inclusion is said to be a 'strict
inclusion'. The set $\{1, 3, 5\}$ is also included in $\{1, 3, 5\}$, but this inclusion is not a
strict inclusion.

Another view of set inclusion is that the set $\{1, 5\}$ is a subset of $\{1, 3, 5\}$. The
set of all subsets of a set is called its 'powerset'. The powerset of $\{1, 3, 5\}$ is

$$\{\{1, 3, 5\}, \{1, 3\}, \{1, 5\}, \{3, 5\}, \{1\}, \{3\}, \{5\}, \{ \}\}$$

Since each member of the set $\{1, 3, 5\}$ is either present or absent in each of the
subsets, the number of subsets is $2^3 = 8$.

There are three binary operations involving sets, which are similar to the
operations of addition, multiplication and subtraction for integers.

The 'union' (or sum) of two sets A and B is that set whose members are

members of either A or B. For example

> let P be the set of all students who can program in Pascal
> and F be the set of all students who can program in Fortran,
> then the union of F and P (F $\cup$ P) is the set of students able to program
> in either Fortran or Pascal or both.

The 'intersection' (or product) of two sets A and B is that set whose members are members of both A and B. If P and F are defined as before, then the intersection of P and F (P $\cap$ F) is that set of students who can program in both Pascal and Fortran.

The 'relative complement' of A with respect to B (written B $-$ A) is that set whose members are members of the set B but are not members of the set A. Again if P and F are defined as before, then P $-$ F is the set of students who can program in Pascal but not in Fortran.

9.2 Sets in Pascal

In set theory, there are no restrictions placed on the type of objects which may be members of a set. In Pascal, only a restricted form of the set data type is available. This both simplifies the language and permits the efficient implementation of sets. In Pascal, the members of a set must all be of the same type, which is the base type of the set. Furthermore the base type must not be a structured type.

The form of the set type definition is shown in figure 9.1, where 'simple type' is any scalar type except REAL.

Figure 9.1

Examples

```
TYPE SOCCERPOSITION  = 1..11;
     VERSATILITY     = SET OF SOCCERPOSITION;
     LIFTBUTTONS     = SET OF FLOOR;

VAR  PLAYER1,PLAYER2 : VERSATILITY;
     BUTTONS         : LIFTBUTTONS;
```

Allowing

```
PLAYER1 := [1]; (* GOALKEEPER *)
PLAYER2 := [7,11]; (* WINGER *)
BUTTONS := [LOWERFIRST,SECOND];
```

In addition to the language restrictions already mentioned, particular implementations are allowed to place a limit on the cardinality of the base type of the sets provided. This limit tends to be between 48 and 256, but more 'generous' implementations of Pascal do exist.

In chapter 7 it was stated that the type of a variable determined that set of values, of which only one could be assumed at any time. So if a variable were declared to be of type 1 .. 3, it could legally adopt one value from the set {1, 2, 3}. If a variable is declared to be of the type **SET OF** 1 .. 3, it may adopt one value from the following set of values

$$\{ \; \{1, 2, 3\}, \{1, 2\}, \{1, 3\}, \{2, 3\}, \{1\}, \{2\}, \{3\}, \{ \; \} \; \}$$

Each of these values is a set, whose elements are members of the base type of the set. This complete set of values is, of course, the powerset of the base type. Consequently the cardinality of a set type in Pascal is

$$2^{(\text{cardinality of base type})}$$

Since sets are processed as a whole in Pascal, as in set theory, there is no set selection operation to break up a set into its components. There is, however, a set constructor. The form of the set constructor is shown in figure 9.2.

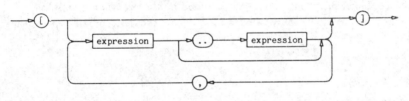

Figure 9.2

Note: In Pascal sets are enclosed between the symbols [and].

The most common form of a set is a series of expressions separated by commas, for example

    ['C', 'E', 'I', 'S']
    [i, j, k + 3]
    [x]
    [1, 3, 5]

If the set consists wholly or partly of a range of values a convenient abbreviation may be used. For example

    [1 .. 5] which is the same as [1, 2, 3, 4, 5]
    [i .. j] which would otherwise need a loop to create it
    ['A' .. 'Z', '0' .. '9']
    [1, 3 .. 10, 18]

Note: If i > j, then [i .. j] denotes the empty set.

The expressions enclosed in a set constructor must all be of the same type, which will be taken as the base type of the set to be constructed. This would appear to mean that the type of the empty set [ ] cannot be deduced because it encloses no expressions. This does not present any real problems because set theory states that the empty set is unique. Consequently the empty set is a member of all set types. Acceptance of this theorem by Pascal necessitates a slight relaxation of the type rules described in chapter 7.

A slightly greater problem is presented by the set [1, 3, 5]. Since its elements are integer expressions, it is clearly of the type **SET OF** INTEGER. Unfortunately the cardinality of the type **SET OF** INTEGER will exceed the restrictions operated by even the most 'generous' Pascal compiler. This difficulty may be overcome by placing a further restriction on the base type of sets. The additional restriction specifies a range of ordinal values which must not be exceeded by the base type of a set. This range usually has a lower bound of zero. With this additional restriction the set [1, 3, 5] may be implicitly converted by the compiler to a set with the appropriate integer subrange base type.

It is an error to attempt to construct a set which violates the implementation restrictions.

Note: In Pascal implementations where this additional restriction has been unacceptable, the problem has been avoided by the provision of suitable predefined functions. These are used to indicate the desired base type of the set.

Set Operations

In addition to the operation of assignment, almost all of the set operations described in the introductory section are provided in Pascal. The exception is the relational operator for strict unclusion, which is not provided but is easily programmed.

There are four relational operators which operate on sets. These are

=		set equality
<>		set inequality
>=	and <=	set inclusion

An additional operator (**IN**) exists, which provides the set membership relation. The second operand of **IN** is a set expression. The first operand is an expression yielding a value of the base type of the set. The result of the relation is true if the value is an element of the set expression.

Notes: (a) The **IN** operator should not be used if the value of the first operand exceeds the range of the base type of the second operand.

(b) All relational operators in Pascal have the same operator precedence.

The membership test is often used in programs to eliminate complicated conditions.

Examples

(1) In the text editor in chapter 8 the following appeared

```
IF (CH = 'E') OR (CH = 'C') OR (CH = 'S') OR (CH = 'I') THEN
```

It is much clearer and more efficient to express this as

```
IF CH IN ['C', 'E', 'I', 'S'] THEN
```

(2) The expression to determine whether a character is a digit or not would normally be

```
(CH >= '0') AND (CH <= '9')
```

Using set membership this is simply

```
CH IN ['0' .. '9']
```

The operations of set union, set difference and set intersection are represented by the symbols +, — and * respectively. Since in Pascal all the members of a set must be of the same type, these operators produce a result of the same type as their operands. The operations of set union and set difference are classified as adding operators and have the same operator precedence as the other adding operators. Similarly the set intersection operator is classified as a multiplying operator.

9.3 A Bingo-Playing Program

Bingo is a game of chance involving any number of players. An additional person is needed to act as the 'caller'. Each player has one rectangular card on which is written a number of different random integers, usually in the range 1 to 90. The cards are all different. The game is played as follows.

Step 1. An integer in the appropriate range is produced in some suitably random manner.

Step 2. The caller announces this number.

Step 3. The players examine their cards and cross out the number called if it appears on their cards.

This process is repeated from step 1 until one or more players observe that all the numbers on their cards have been crossed out. The player(s) who cause the game to end have won the game. The problem is to write a program which simulates the game of bingo. The numbers which are to be 'called' may be read from the file INPUT.

The over-all structure of the program must be

```
PROGRAM EX9A(INPUT,OUTPUT,PLAYERS);
BEGIN
(* INITIALISE *)
REPEAT
  (* CALL A NUMBER *)
  (* CHECK FOR BINGO *)
UNTIL BINGO
END.
```

The key to the elegant and efficient solution of many programming problems lies in the choice of the data structures. The first data structure to be considered is the bingo card. Although a bingo card is rectangular and matrix-like, the arrangement of the numbers on the card has no significance. A bingo card is simply a collection of numbers. The operations which may be needed are

(1) determining whether the number called is on a card
(2) crossing-out (removal) of numbers
(3) detecting a completely crossed-out card (empty collection).

The correct choice of data structure for a bingo card is clearly the set. This gives

```
CONST CARDLIMIT = 90;
TYPE BINGONUMBER  = 1..CARDLIMIT;
     BINGOCARD    = SET OF BINGONUMBER;
```

All the players taken together may be regarded as a set of bingo cards. However, Pascal does not allow such data types because the base type, BINGOCARD, is structured. Even if it did, the cardinality of such a type would be rather large. Since the operations of number removal and bingo detection are to be performed for every player and the order in which the players are simulated is of no consequence, it is easiest to process the players in the same order every time. So, all the players may be represented by a sequence of bingo cards

```
TYPE  BINGOPLAYERS = FILE OF BINGOCARD;
```

This choice has a disadvantage. As each number is called it must be crossed out (removed) from the cards on which it occurs. This means that a new sequence of bingo cards must be produced, with this number removed, for use when the next number is called.

This disadvantage may be simply avoided by ignoring the way in which a human player operates. A player is in a winning position when the set of numbers already called includes all those on his bingo card. This approach requires the creation of a set of 'numbers already called', but means that the sequence of bingo cards need only be *scanned* for each number called. The complete program may now be written easily.

```
PROGRAM EX9A(INPUT,OUTPUT,PLAYERS);
CONST CARDLIMIT = 90;
TYPE BINGONUMBER  = 1..CARDLIMIT;
     BINGOCARD    = SET OF BINGONUMBER;
     BINGOPLAYERS = FILE OF BINGOCARD;
VAR  PLAYERS : BINGOPLAYERS;
     CARD,NUMBERSCALLED : BINGOCARD;
     NUMBER  : BINGONUMBER;
     BINGO   : BOOLEAN;
     PLAYERNUMBER : 0..MAXINT;
BEGIN
(* INITIALISE *)
NUMBERSCALLED := [];
BINGO := FALSE;
REPEAT
  (* CALL A NUMBER *)
  READ(NUMBER);
  NUMBERSCALLED := NUMBERSCALLED + [NUMBER];
  (* CHECK FOR BINGO *)
  RESET(PLAYERS); PLAYERNUMBER := 0;
  WHILE NOT EOF(PLAYERS) DO
    BEGIN
    READ(PLAYERS,CARD);
    PLAYERNUMBER := PLAYERNUMBER + 1;
    IF NUMBERSCALLED >= CARD THEN
      BEGIN
      WRITELN(' BINGO FOR PLAYER NUMBER ',PLAYERNUMBER);
      BINGO := TRUE
      END
    END
UNTIL BINGO
END.
```

A Postscript

Since the set data type in Pascal exhibits both language and implementation restrictions, there will be circumstances in which the logical data structure to use is the set, but one will be prevented from doing so. In such circumstances other data structures must be used to provide the set data structure. A general discussion of the topic is beyond the scope of this text. Interested readers are referred to Coleman (1978), Dahl *et al.* (1972) and Aho *et al.* (1974).

Exercises

9.1 List all the members of the following sets
(a) SET OF (RED, GREEN, BLUE);
(b) SET OF 1 . . 4;

9.2 Evaluate the following set expressions
(a) [1 . . 4] * [3, 5]
(b) [1 . . 4] + [3, 5]
(c) [1 . . 4] − [3, 5]

9.3 Which of the following boolean expressions yield TRUE?
(a) [1, 2, 3] = [1 . . 3]
(b) [1, 2, 3] <= [1 . . 3]
(c) [0, 1, 2] <= [2, 3]
(d) 5 IN [0. . 3, 4 . . 8]

Problems

9.1 Write a program to find prime numbers using the sieve of Eratosthenes. Briefly the method is as follows.

>Put all the numbers to be considered into the sieve.
>**REPEAT**
>   Find and remove from the sieve the smallest remaining number; this is a prime number.
>   Remove from the sieve all multiples of this prime number.
>**UNTIL** the sieve is empty.

You should use a set to represent the sieve. (Unless a 'generous' implementation of Pascal is available, the use of a set will severely limit this program.)

9.2 Modify the program created above to use a file of sets to represent the sieve.

10 Elementary Structured Types 2—the Array

10.1 An Introduction to Arrays

The array data type will be introduced by contrasting it with the sequential file. The array data type is like the sequential file type in that in each case their components must all be of the same type. Unlike a sequential file, however, an array has a fixed number of components which are all equally accessible. Consequently the components of an array may be accessed randomly. In particular, to alter the value of an array variable it is not necessary to produce a complete, new value for the array since the appropriate components may be selectively updated.

To select a component of an array variable the name of the variable is subscripted by an index, which is an expression enclosed in square brackets. This expression must yield a value of the index type of the array. A simplified form of the array type specification, which defines both the index type and the base type of an array, is shown in figure 10.1.

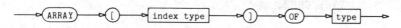

Figure 10.1

Notes: (a) The form of 'type', which determines the base type of the array, is given in full in appendix I.
(b) The index type may be any scalar type except REAL.

The number of components in an array is determined by the cardinality of the index type, since there is one component of the array for each value of the index type. Consequently the cardinality of an array type is

$$\text{cardinality of base type}^{(\text{cardinality of index type})}$$

Example

```
TYPE ALFA = ARRAY[1..10] OF CHAR;
VAR  A     : ALFA;
     C     : CHAR;
     I     : 1..10;
```

All variables of the type ALFA have ten components. Each of these components is itself a variable, in this case of the type CHAR.

The selection of the component of an ALFA variable is achieved by using, as an index expression, any expression which yields a value in the range of the index type. For example

```
I := 5;
A[3] := 'X';
C := A[I-2];
```

If the index expression yields a value outside the required range then the program is in error. All respectable Pascal implementations will detect such errors and produce a suitable diagnostic message.

Apart from the selection operation, the only operations defined in Pascal for entire arrays are those of assignment and equality.†

10.2   Arrays of Arrays

The base type of an array may be any data type. In particular, it may be another array. This results in a multidimensional array. For example

```
TYPE CHESSBOARD = ARRAY[1..8] OF ARRAY[1..8] OF CHESSPIECE;
     CUBE       = ARRAY[SIZE] OF ARRAY[SIZE] OF
                         ARRAY[SIZE] OF REAL;
VAR  BOARD : CHESSBOARD;
     SOLID : CUBE;
```

If an array selector is applied to a multidimensional array variable, the resulting variable, for example, BOARD [3], is another array which itself may be indexed, for example, BOARD [3] [5]. Similarly one, two or three array selectors may be used with the variable CUBE, for example, CUBE [I] [J] [K].

The array type specification does in fact permit a considerable simplification of the definition of multidimensional arrays. The full form of the array type specification is shown in figure 10.2.

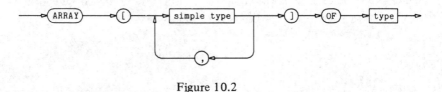

Figure 10.2

---

†Several important Pascal compilers do not currently implement equality on entire arrays, but the majority of compilers do. The intention of the creator of Pascal is, unfortunately, not clear from the Revised Report.

Consequently the definition of CHESSBOARD and CUBE may be contracted to

```
TYPE CHESSBOARD = ARRAY[1..8,1..8] OF CHESSPIECE;
     CUBE       = ARRAY[SIZE,SIZE,SIZE] OF REAL;
```

A similar abbreviation is also provided for the application of more than one array selector.

BOARD [3, 5] is equivalent to BOARD [3] [5]
CUBE [1, 8, 2] is equivalent to CUBE [1] [8] [2]

Although it is considered to be good style to either use both these abbreviations or neither, the language does not impose such restrictions.

It is, of course, possible to define multidimensional arrays in terms of previously declared array data types. For example

```
TYPE VECTOR = ARRAY[1..N] OF REAL;
     MATRIX = ARRAY[1..N] OF VECTOR;
VAR  V : VECTOR; M : MATRIX;
```

In this case all of the following assignments are legal

```
V[I]    := M[I,J] + 1.5;
M[I][J] := V[I] + V[J];
V       := M[I];
M[J]    := V;
```

10.3 Arrays of CHAR

The character string, which is a sequence of characters, is frequently needed in programming. Unfortunately the character string, like the sequential file, is a data type of infinite cardinality. In many cases it is possible to give a realistic upper limit for the lengths of all the character strings in a program. In these circumstances fixed-length character strings will suffice. In Pascal the fixed-length character string may be represented by a packed array of characters. So, if in a program an upper limit of twenty is reasonable, the type STRING could be defined as

```
TYPE STRING = PACKED ARRAY[1..20] OF CHAR;
```

Variables of the type STRING may be used in the same way as any other arrays. They may be assigned and subscripted. To facilitate the use of packed arrays of characters as fixed-length strings, all six relational operations are defined.

Notes: (a) Only equal length strings may be compared.
(b) The ordering of two strings is defined by the lexicographic ordering of the strings, for example

> 'ABCD' < 'ABCE' is true
> 'BAA' > 'ADD' is true

(c) The lexicographic ordering is based on the ordering of values of the type CHAR, which is implementation dependent.

String constants, which were introduced in chapter 5, are taken to be of the type **PACKED ARRAY** [1 .. N] **OF** CHAR, where N $(N > 1)$ is the length of the string. These constants may be assigned to or compared with any compatible array type. So the following is legal

```
TYPE STRING = PACKED ARRAY[1..15] OF CHAR;
     NAME   = PACKED ARRAY[1..20] OF CHAR;
VAR  N : NAME;
     S : STRING;
     .
     .
N := 'THIS IS TWENTY CHARS';
S := 'THIS IS FIFTEEN';
```

Note: A string variable will be compatible with a string constant if
(a) the index type is a subrange of integer
(b) the lower bound of the index type is one
(c) the cardinality of the index type is the same as the length of the string.

10.4 Packing and Unpacking

Although a packed array may be used in the same way as an unpacked array, the selection mechanism will probably be less efficient. In some cases this overhead can be reduced by copying the packed array into an unpacked one before using it. This cannot be achieved by simply using an assignment statement since the two arrays will be of incompatible types.

Assuming

```
TYPE THING = ...... ;
VAR  A  : ARRAY[M..N] OF THING;
     PA : PACKED ARRAY[U..V] OF THING;
     J  : U..V;
```

and that $N - M \geqslant V - U$, the programmer can solve the problem thus

```
FOR J := U TO V DO A[J-U+M] := PA[J];
```

This, of course, requires that every element of the packed array be selected. In Pascal a standard procedure called UNPACK is provided which is similar in effect to the statement above. It also provides the implementor of any Pascal system with an opportunity to make this operation more efficient.

With the same assumptions as before, the procedure UNPACK is defined such that UNPACK(PA, A, I) is equivalent to

```
FOR J := U TO V DO A[J-U+I] := PA[J];
```

A similar procedure called PACK is also available. PACK(A, I, PA) is equivalent to

```
FOR J := U TO V DO PA[J] := A[J-U+I];
```

Notes: (a) The **FOR** loop variable, J, is local to the UNPACK/PACK procedure.
(b) The starting point in the unpacked array is a parameter of the procedure.
(c) The parameters of PACK and UNPACK are not in the same order.
(d) UNPACK will not accept a string constant as a parameter.

10.5 The Array in Use

The array is the most versatile of the structured data types in Pascal. It may be used in a variety of different ways, which suggests that the array has a rather mixed mathematical ancestry.

10.5.1 *n-tuples*

The term n-tuple is used in mathematics to describe an ordered sequence of n values, which are not necessarily different and not necessarily of the same type. The array may only be used to represent an n-tuple when all the values are of the same type. Furthermore the array is the correct choice if and only if the components of the n-tuple are to be processed in a similar way or the order of the component values is to be permuted. If this is not the case, then the record data type should be used (see chapter 11). The vector and the matrix are classic examples of n-tuples for which the array is the correct data type.

A Scalar Product Procedure

The scalar product, SP, of two vectors, V and W, is defined as

$$SP = \sum_{i=1}^{n} V_i * W_i$$

Since the scalar product is a single value, a function should be used. The heading for the function might be

```
FUNCTION SCALARPRODUCT(VAR V,W : VECTOR) : REAL;
```

where the type VECTOR has previously been defined by

```
CONST N = ..... ;
TYPE  VECTOR = ARRAY[1..N] OF REAL;
```

the complete function is

```
FUNCTION SCALARPRODUCT(VAR V,W : VECTOR) : REAL;
  VAR I : 1..N;
      SP : REAL;
  BEGIN
  SP := 0;
  FOR I := 1 TO N DO
    SP := SP + V[I] * W[I];
  SCALARPRODUCT := SP
  END;
```

Note that a local variable must be used to accumulate the scalar product, since the use of a function identifier in an expression will invoke the function itself.

10.5.2 Sequences of Fixed Length

The choice of data structures often has a significant effect on the quality of a program. Frequently when the logical choice is an advanced data structure, the introduction of some reasonable restrictions will permit the use of an elementary data structure. A sequence with a size restriction may be replaced by an array. The use of arrays of CHAR as strings is a particular example of this. When the decision to use an elementary data structure has been made, further simplifications may then be possible.

Sequential Searching

A sequential search is the name used to describe the operation of examining each item of a sequence in turn to determine whether it is the same as the interrogating value or not. An obvious scheme for this is

```
(*INITIALISE*)
REPEAT
  (* ADVANCE *)
UNTIL (* ITEM FOUND OR END OF SEQUENCE *)
```

In Pascal this might be

Using an array	*Using a file*

```
I := 0;                              RESET(SEQ);
REPEAT                               REPEAT
  I := I + 1                           READ(SEQ,X)
UNTIL (A[I] = NEEDED) OR (I = N);    UNTIL (X = NEEDED) OR EOF(SEQ);
FOUND := A[I] = NEEDED;              FOUND := X = NEEDED;
```

The array search may be improved by the use of a sentinel value stored in an additional component of the array. This results in the following simplified scheme

```
A[N+1] := NEEDED; I := 0;
REPEAT
  I := I + 1
UNTIL A[I] = NEEDED;
FOUND := I <> N + 1;
```

Note: Sequential searching is a simple searching method. It may not be appropriate to use it in an application which is dominated by searching. A more complex, but faster, method should be substituted [Knuth, 1973; Wirth, 1975*b*].

10.5.3 Mapping Functions

A function is a rule which specifies a transformation between two sets of values. If certain restrictions are applied, then an array may be used to describe a function. The term mapping function will be used in this case, to distinguish it from a functional procedure.

Factorial

Undeniably the best way to compute a factorial is to use a mapping function — the program simply looks up the answer in a table. A suitable declaration for the table is

```
VAR   FACTORIAL : ARRAY[0..N] OF 1..MAXINT;
```

where N is the largest integer whose factorial is $\leqslant$ MAXINT. The value of N is, in fact, remarkably small. The actual value will depend on MAXINT. Some typical values are

N	MAXINT
7	32767
10	8388607
12	2147483647
16	281474976710655

The table can easily be initialised, as follows

```
F := 1; FACTORIAL[0] := 1;
FOR I := 1 TO N DO
  BEGIN
  F := F * I; FACTORIAL[I] := F
  END;
```

Inversion

The clarity gained by the use of enumerated scalar types is offset by an inability to manipulate the values arithmetically. In some circumstances this presents a problem. Consider a simple board game. The players could be designated 0 and 1 or BLACK and WHITE. The latter is to be preferred.

```
TYPE COLOUR = (BLACK,WHITE);
VAR  PLAYER : COLOUR;
     P      : 0..1;
```

The problem is to form an expression which will represent the other player. When integers were used this would simply be $(1 - P)$, but arithmetic operations cannot be applied to enumerated scalars. The solution is

```
VAR  OTHER : ARRAY[COLOUR] OF COLOUR;
```

This will be initialised thus

```
OTHER[BLACK] := WHITE; OTHER[WHITE] := BLACK;
```

Conversion

Mapping functions may also be used to convert values of one type into values of another.

For example, if a problem requires that enumerated scalar values are to be output as text, then they need to be converted into strings. A suitable data structure for this purpose would be

```
VAR  CONV : ARRAY[COLOUR] OF PACKED ARRAY[1..5] OF CHAR;
```

which would be initialised as

```
CONV[WHITE] := 'WHITE'; CONV[BLACK] := 'BLACK';
```

The opposite conversion, from strings to scalars, cannot be done using a mapping function since strings may not be used as indices. The above data structure could be searched sequentially to perform the conversion. Those Pascal implementations which have been extended to permit textual input and output of enumerated scalars, perform the task in a similar way.

Exercises

10.1 A sequence of characters is held on a file of CHAR. Define a type which is suitable for holding the frequency count of each letter in the sequence. Write a Pascal program to store the frequency count in the data structure.

10.2 Define a type suitable for noting the existence of every different two-character sequence which occurs in a sequence of characters held on a file.

Problems

10.1 Rewrite the program which calculates prime numbers, to use an array of sets. Compare this program with the 'file of sets' version.

10.2 Write a procedure which will compute the frequencies of all 'digrams' (two letter pairs) which occur in a piece of text held on a file. Then write a procedure which will print out the data structure containing these frequencies. You may assume that the alphabetic characters are contiguous.

10.3 Modify your solution to problem 10.2 to allow for the fact that the alphabetic characters may not be contiguous. You should use either a set or a mapping function for this purpose.

11 Elementary Structured Types 3—the Record

11.1 An Introduction to Records

The record data type is an n-tuple. It has a fixed number of components which may be of different types. This ability to form a structure from elements of arbitrary types means that the record is the most general structured type in Pascal.

Both arrays and records may be used to represent n-tuples, so a comparison of their properties is appropriate. The essential difference between the two structured types is to be found in the restrictions on their components. All the components of an array must be of the same type, whereas a record may have components of different types. This reflects itself in the selection mechanisms available. The type rules of Pascal, described in chapter 7, require that the type of any component selected from a structure should be known without the execution of the program. Hence, because there may be several different component types in a record, a computed selector is not allowed. Instead, each component is given a name, which is used to select it. A computed selector may be used with arrays. In all other respects records and arrays are similar. They are both random access structures which may be selectively updated. In both cases, the cardinality of the structured type is the product of the cardinalities of the component types.

11.2 Records in Pascal

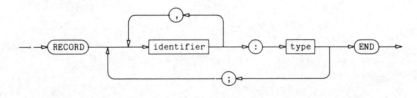

Figure 11.1

A simplified form of the record specification is shown in figure 11.1, where the full form of 'type', which may be any type, is given in appendix I.

Examples

```
TYPE COMPLEX   = RECORD
                   RE,IM : REAL
                   END;
     STRING    = PACKED ARRAY[1..N] OF CHAR;
     FULLNAME  = RECORD
                   SURNAME     : STRING;
                   NOOFFNAMES  : 1..3;
                   FORENAMES   : ARRAY[1..3] OF STRING
                   END;
     MONTH     = (JAN,FEB,MAR,APR,MAY,JUN,
                   JLY,AUG,SEP,OCT,NOV,DEC);
     DATE      = RECORD
                   D : 1..31;
                   M : MONTH;
                   Y : 1901..2000
                   END;
     HOLIDAYS  = ARRAY[1..K] OF DATE;
```

RE, IM, SURNAME, NOOFFNAMES, D, M and Y are all record components. Such components are called 'fields'. All the field identifiers within a record type must be unique, since they form part of the selection operation. The field identifiers ought to be different from all the other identifiers declared in the same block, but this is not essential since the scope of a field identifier is very restricted. The scope of a field identifier is

(1) the smallest record definition containing it, and
(2) all selectors referring to a record variable of the appropriate type.

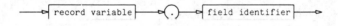

Figure 11.2

The components of a record are selected by using field designators. The form of a field designator is shown in figure 11.2, where the 'record variable' may be a component of a structure.

Examples

Given the declarations

```
VAR GIRL      : FULLNAME;
    BIRTHDAY  : DATE;
    STATUTORY : HOLIDAYS;
```

the following are all legal.

```
BIRTHDAY.D := 8;
BIRTHDAY.M := NOV;
BIRTHDAY.Y := 1973;
GIRL.FORENAMES[1] := 'REBECCA   ';
GIRL.FORENAMES[2] := 'ANN       ';
GIRL.NOOFFNAMES   := 2;
GIRL.SURNAME      := 'ADDYMAN   ';
STATUTORY[I].Y := 1977;
STATUTORY[I].M := DEC;
STATUTORY[I].D := 25;
```

Apart from the selection operation the only operations which are defined in
Pascal for entire records are those of assignment and equality.†

11.3   The WITH Statement

Structured data types encourage the creation of variables whose components
are logically related. A natural consequence of this will be that the components
are processed as a group. The components of a file or an array may be processed
concisely by using the repetition statements. The elements of a set are always
processed together. With records, however, the diversity of component types
and the lack of a computed selector means that the components of a record will
be processed by a sequence of statements. For example, given

```
TYPE PERSON = RECORD
              NAME     : FULLNAME;
              BIRTHDAY : DATE
              END;
VAR  DAUGHTER : PERSON;
```

DAUGHTER could be initialised as follows

```
DAUGHTER.NAME.SURNAME      := 'ADDYMAN   ';
DAUGHTER.NAME.NOOFFNAMES   := 2;
DAUGHTER.NAME.FORENAMES[1] := 'SARAH     ';
DAUGHTER.NAME.FORENAMES[2] := 'MARIE     ';
DAUGHTER.BIRTHDAY.D := 4;
DAUGHTER.BIRTHDAY.M := NOV;
DAUGHTER.BIRTHDAY.Y := 1975;
```

But this would have been much shorter if several separate variables had been
declared and initialised thus

```
DSURNAME      := 'ADDYMAN   ';
DFORENAMES[1] := 'SARAH     ';
DFORENAMES[2] := 'MARIE     ';
```

†See note in chapter 10 on array equality.

Using the **WITH** statement it is possible to access the components of a record as if they were simple variables. The form of the **WITH** statement is shown in figure 11.3.

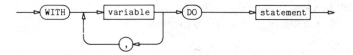

Figure 11.3

The **WITH** statement effectively extends the scope of the field identifiers of the records listed. As a consequence, within the qualified statement they may be accessed with the simplicity and efficiency of local variables. The following **WITH** statement has the same effect as the seven assignments given earlier.

```
WITH DAUGHTER,NAME,BIRTHDAY DO
  BEGIN
  SURNAME        := 'ADDYMAN    ';
  FORENAMES[1]   := 'SARAH      ';
  FORENAMES[2]   := 'MARIE      ';
  NOOFNAMES      := 2;
  D := 4; M := NOV; Y := 1975
  END;
```

Notes: (a) The statement **WITH A, B DO S**; is equivalent to

> **WITH A DO**
>   **WITH B DO S**;

So the second record variable (B) may be a component of the first record variable (A), as in the example above.

(b) The field identifiers which have been exposed by the **WITH** statement, for example, SURNAME, prevent the same identifiers being used for different purposes within the **WITH** statement.

(c) No assignments may be made by the qualified statement to elements of the record variable list, for example, DAUGHTER, NAME and BIRTHDAY in the previous example.

11.4 A Simple Application of Records—A Card Game

The problem is as follows. Several players are dealt one card each. The input to the program will be this deal, presented in the form

	card face	card suit	name of the player (right justified)
for example	4S		WILLIAMS
	AC		RODGERS
	0D		BLOGGS

The names will not exceed twenty characters in length. The characters 'OD' represent the ten of diamonds.

The program will scan this input and print out the highest and second highest cards with their player's names. The normal values of cards will apply. The ace will be high. If two cards have the same face value, the suit will be used to decide the higher card on the basis that

$$\text{spades} > \text{hearts} > \text{diamonds} > \text{clubs}$$

The over-all structure of the program could be

```
PROGRAM EX11A(INPUT,OUTPUT);
BEGIN
(* INITIALISE *)
WHILE NOT EOF DO
  BEGIN
  (* READ CARD AND NAME *)
  IF (* A VALID CARD *) THEN
    BEGIN (* PROCESS A CARD *)
    IF (* HIGHER THAN FIRST *) THEN
      (* NEW FIRST AND SECOND *)
    ELSE IF (* HIGHER THAN SECOND *) THEN
            (* NEW SECOND *)
    END
  ELSE (* ERROR *)
  END;
(* WRITE RESULTS *)
END.
```

An examination of this scheme suggests the need for a type

```
TYPE CARDFACE       = RECORD
                      FACE : CHAR;
                      SUIT : CHAR
                      END;
```

Associated with each card is a player's name, so another record type will be needed

```
TYPE CARDANDPLAYER = RECORD
                     CARD : CARDFACE;
                     NAME : STRING
                     END;
```

The following variables will certainly be needed

```
VAR CANDP,FIRST,SECOND : CARDANDPLAYER;
```

Reading the card and the player's name is simply

```
WITH CANDP.CARD DO READ(FACE,SUIT);
FOR I := 1 TO N DO READ(CANDP.NAME[I]);
READLN;
```

The validation is also straightforward if sets are used. The validation is

```
WITH CANDP,CARD DO
   IF (FACE IN ['0','2'..'9','J','Q','K','A']) AND
      (SUIT IN ['C','D','H','S']) THEN
      BEGIN (* PROCESS A CARD *)
        .
        .
      END
   ELSE WRITELN('INVALID CARD ',FACE,SUIT)
```

We postulate the existence of a function whose heading is

```
FUNCTION HIGHER(A,B : CARDFACE) : BOOLEAN;
```

which yields TRUE if A is higher than the B. Given this function and the enclosing **WITH** statement, the heart of the loop can be written as follows

```
IF HIGHER(CARD,FIRST.CARD) THEN
   BEGIN
   SECOND := FIRST; FIRST := CANDP
   END
ELSE IF HIGHER(CARD,SECOND.CARD) THEN SECOND := CANDP
```

All that remains now is to write this function.

The ordering of suits is the same as their alphabetic ordering, but the ordering of the face values is unrelated to the ordering of their character representations. It will therefore be necessary to convert the face values encoded as characters into a set of values which represent their true ordering. Such a set of values is defined by the type

```
TYPE RANK = (TWO,THREE,FOUR,FIVE,SIX,SEVEN,EIGHT,NINE,TEN,
             JACK,QUEEN,KING,ACE);
```

The conversion can be performed by using a mapping function based on a variable of the type **ARRAY [CHAR] OF RANK**, which has been suitably initialised. Since the array will only be accessed with valid characters, the majority of the entries in the mapping function can be left undefined. To avoid initialising the mapping function on every activation of the HIGHER function, the initialisation may be moved into the main program at the cost of offending the over-all design structure. This difficulty can be satisfactorily resolved in a language with structured constants or with more complex scope rules.

The complete program is

```
PROGRAM EX11A(INPUT,OUTPUT);
CONST N = 10;
TYPE RANK = (TWO,THREE,FOUR,FIVE,SIX,SEVEN,EIGHT,NINE,TEN,
             JACK,QUEEN,KING,ACE);
     STRING = PACKED ARRAY[1..N] OF CHAR;
     CARDFACE = RECORD
                   FACE : CHAR;
                   SUIT : CHAR
                END;
     CARDANDPLAYER = RECORD
                        CARD : CARDFACE;
                        NAME : STRING
                     END;
VAR VALUE : ARRAY[CHAR] OF RANK;
    CANDP,FIRST,SECOND : CARDANDPLAYER;
    I : 1..N;
FUNCTION HIGHER(A,B : CARDFACE) : BOOLEAN;
  BEGIN
  HIGHER := FALSE;
  IF VALUE[A.FACE] > VALUE[B.FACE] THEN HIGHER := TRUE
  ELSE IF VALUE[A.FACE] = VALUE[B.FACE] THEN
          HIGHER := A.SUIT >= B.SUIT
  END; (* HIGHER *)
BEGIN
(* INITIALISE *)
WITH FIRST,CARD DO
  BEGIN
  FACE := '2'; SUIT := 'C'; NAME := '          '
  END;
SECOND := FIRST;
(* SET UP MAPPING FUNCTION *)
VALUE['2'] := TWO;   VALUE['3'] := THREE;VALUE['4'] := FOUR;
VALUE['5'] := FIVE; VALUE['6'] := SIX;   VALUE['7'] := SEVEN;
VALUE['8'] := EIGHT;VALUE['9'] := NINE; VALUE['0'] := TEN;
VALUE['J'] := JACK; VALUE['Q'] := QUEEN;VALUE['K'] := KING;
VALUE['A'] := ACE;
WHILE NOT EOF DO
  BEGIN
  (* READ CARD AND NAME *)
  WITH CANDP.CARD DO READ(FACE,SUIT);
  FOR I := 1 TO N DO READ(CANDP.NAME[I]);
  READLN;
  WITH CANDP,CARD DO
    IF (FACE IN ['0','2'..'9','J','Q','K','A']) AND
       (SUIT IN ['C','D','H','S']) THEN
      BEGIN(* PROCESS A CARD *)
      IF HIGHER(CARD,FIRST.CARD) THEN
        BEGIN
        SECOND := FIRST; FIRST := CANDP
        END
      ELSE IF HIGHER(CARD,SECOND.CARD) THEN SECOND := CANDP
      END
    ELSE WRITELN('INVALID CARD ',FACE,SUIT)
  END;
```

```
(* WRITE RESULTS *)
WITH FIRST,CARD DO
  WRITELN('THE WINNER IS ',NAME,' WITH ',FACE,SUIT);
WITH SECOND,CARD DO
  WRITELN('THE SECOND IS ',NAME,' WITH ',FACE,SUIT)
END.
```

Exercises

11.1 Write a function which will calculate the number of days between two dates. The heading for the function will be

```
FUNCTION DIFFERENCE(D1,D2 : DATE) : INTEGER;
```

11.2 Modify the output of the card program so that the card values are more presentable. For example the output could be

THE WINNER IS WILLIAMS WITH THE ACE OF CLUBS
THE SECOND IS BLOGGS WITH THE QUEEN OF DIAMONDS

The output should not include any redundant spaces.

Problem

Write a program which will input one or more lines of text and output the equivalent in Morse code. The conversion from characters to Morse code should read from the file on which they are held into a more suitable data structure. The information on tne Morse code file is of the following form

    symbol to be coded-spaces-length of Morse code-spaces-Morse code

for example

A	2	. —
E	1	.

  etc.

In the encoded form of the message, each letter must be separated from the next by one space only. Each word should appear on a separate line.
Notes: (a) The longest Morse code representation of any symbol is six mixed dots and dashes.
(b) Your program should reject any character for which a Morse code equivalent is not provided.

A typical form of input and output could be as follows.

```
A ROSE OVEN SPOON


  . -
  . - .  - - -   . . .   .
  - - -   . . . -  .  - .
  . . .  . - - .  - - -   - - -   - .
```

12 Elementary Structured Types 4—the Variant

12.1 The Need for Type Unions

Using the four structuring methods which have been described, a programmer may create an infinite variety of structured types. All of these types have one thing in common. For any given structured type, all the variables must have an identical structure. There is, however, a wide range of applications for which these structures are inadequate because the data structures must describe objects whose characteristics may vary.

An Example

Consider the following three geometric shapes: a rectangle, a triangle and a circle. A rectangular shape may be described by its height and its width thus

```
TYPE RECTANGLE = RECORD
                   HEIGHT : REAL;
                   WIDTH  : REAL
                 END;
```

A triangle, however, cannot be described unambiguously in this way. A suitable type for a triangle might be

```
TYPE TRIANGLE  = RECORD
                   SIDE1,SIDE2 : REAL;
                   ANGLE : REAL
                 END;
```

A circle may be adequately described by its radius.

How should the type GEOMETRICFIGURE be defined?

A variable of the type RECTANGLE may assume any of the values of the type RECTANGLE. Similarly, a variable of the type TRIANGLE may assume any of the values of the type TRIANGLE, etc. A variable of the type GEOMETRICFIGURE must be able to assume any of the values of any of the three geometric figures. So the set of values which constitutes the type GEOMETRICFIGURE is the union of the sets of values of the types RECTANGLE, TRIANGLE and CIRCLE.

In the above example, the three types which were to be united had no components in common. It is more usual to unite types which have some common components. In this case, the type is considered to have several 'variants'. Many examples of the second kind of structure may be discovered by considering the personal details of individuals. A structure which is related to a person's occupation might contain

Common Information	—	full name and date of birth
Variants		
employed	—	name of the employer
self-employed	—	whether the person is also an employer, and if so the number of employees
unemployed	—·	the date on which the unemployment was registered
retired	—	the date of retirement
housewife	—	name of husband, date of marriage
student	—	place of education, date of start of course, if a graduate then the research topic, otherwise the course code

Since the variant is more common than the simple type union, the term variant is used in Pascal. All the variant types in Pascal are record variants.

12.2   Record Variants in Pascal

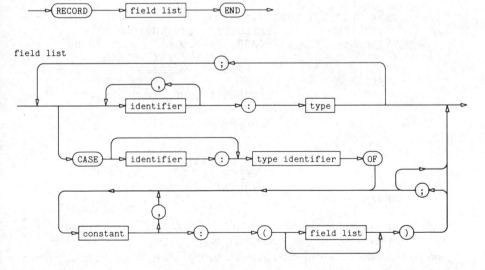

Figure 12.1

It is not possible to determine which variant is being assumed, at any time, by a variable of variant type, without executing the program. Since the variant assumed by a variable may change during the execution of a program, it is necessary to remember which variant is currently active. The most natural place for this information is within the structure itself. This discriminating information is saved in an additional field of the record known as the 'tag field'. It is the need for a tag field which causes the variant type to be based on the record type in Pascal.

The full form of the record type specification is shown in figure 12.1.

Examples

```
TYPE FIGURE            = (RECT,TRI,CIRC);
     GEOMETRICFIGURE = RECORD
                         CASE KIND : FIGURE OF
                           RECT : (WIDTH,HEIGHT : REAL);
                           CIRC : (RADIUS : REAL);
                           TRI  : (SIDE1,SIDE2,ANGLE : REAL)
                         END;
     EMPLSTATUS      = (EMPLOYED,UNEMPLOYED,SELFEMPLOYED,
                         RETIRED,HOUSEWIFE,STUDENT);
     POSINT          = 0 .. MAXINT;
     (* FULLNAME , DATE AND STRING
        ARE DEFINED IN CHAPTER 11 *)
     EMPLOYDETAILS   =
       RECORD
       NAME : FULLNAME;
       BIRTHDAY : DATE;
       CASE STATUS : EMPLSTATUS OF
         EMPLOYED      : (EMPLOYER : STRING);
         SELFEMPLOYED : ( CASE ISEMPLOYER : BOOLEAN OF
                           TRUE : (NOOFEMPLOYEES : POSINT);
                           FALSE: ( )    );
         RETIRED,
         UNEMPLOYED    : (DATEREGISTERED : DATE);
         HOUSEWIFE     : (HUSBAND : FULLNAME;
                         MARRIAGEDATE : DATE);
         STUDENT       : (COLLEGE : STRING;
                         STARTDATE : DATE
                         CASE GRADUATE : BOOLEAN OF
                           TRUE : (TOPIC : STRING);
                           FALSE: (COURSE : POSINT)    )
       END;
```

Although the date field in the UNEMPLOYED and RETIRED variants refers to different events, the variants have been combined for convenience. *Notes*: (a) All the field identifiers must be distinct, even if they are in different variants of the same record.

(b) The fixed part of a 'field list' precedes the variant part.

(c) In a variant, the parentheses must be present, even if they will enclose nothing.

(d) A record variable with variants is never compatible with a record variable without variants. In particular the following assignment is illegal, even if G.KIND = TRI.

```
VAR   T : TRIANGLE;
      G : GEOMETRICFIGURE;
   .
   .
   .
   G := T; (* IS ILLEGAL *)
```

(e) The type of the tag field(s) must be specified by type identifier(s).
(f) The type of the tag field may be any scalar type except real.
(g) The variant part of field list ought not to include any components of the type **FILE**.

12.3   Using Record Variants

Variables which are record variants cannot be processed safely unless their tag fields are correctly set. Since the maintenance of tag field values is the responsibility of the programmer and not of the Pascal system, additional care should be exercised when writing or modifying programs which use record variants. The fields of a particular variant should only be accessed when the tag field has the appropriate value.

A detailed inspection of the syntax of a record definition reveals the fact that tag field identifiers may be omitted. Record variants which do not have tag fields are known as 'free unions'. Those which have tag fields are called 'discriminated unions'. Fortunately, free-unions are necessary for only a few applications. They are principally used when either

(1) discriminating information is stored elsewhere and the space occupied by the tag fields cannot be spared; or
(2) machine - dependent programs are being written. An example of such a program is one which will create an equivalent assembly language program by processing the bit patterns in the memory of the computer.

Since the use of free unions is infrequent, and the likelihood of an error is high, many Pascal implementations insist that the tag field be present.

Warning   Free unions should only be used by experienced programmers.

12.4   Calculating the Area of a Geometric Figure

The problem is to write a function whose result will be the area of the geometric figure. A suitable heading is

```
FUNCTION AREA(FIG : GEOMETRICFIGURE) : REAL;
```

The actual calculation involved is completely different for each kind of figure. A **CASE** statement will be used to select the appropriate calculation for each variant. This results in the following encoding for the function.

```
FUNCTION AREA(FIG : GEOMETRICFIGURE) : REAL;
  CONST PI = 3.1415926536;
  BEGIN
  WITH FIG DO
    CASE KIND OF
      RECT : AREA := HEIGHT * WIDTH;
      CIRC : AREA := PI * SQR(RADIUS);
      TRI  : AREA := 0.5 * SIDE1 * SIDE2 * SIN(ANGLE)
    END
  END;
```

Exercises

12.1 Write a function whose heading is

```
FUNCTION PERIMETER(FIG : GEOMETRICFIGURE) : REAL;
```

to calculate the perimeter of a geometric figure.

12.2 Assuming that FULLNAME is defined as in chapter 11, and that

```
TYPE FEMALESTUDENT = RECORD
                     NAME : FULLNAME;
                     SIZE : ARRAY[1..3] OF 400..1299
                     END;
     MALESTUDENT   = RECORD
                     NAME : FULLNAME;
                     MONEY : REAL;
                     CAR : BOOLEAN
                     END;
```

(a) Write a program to compute the average size of the persons described on the file **VAR** GIRLS: **FILE OF** FEMALESTUDENT;
(b) Write a program to compute the average amount of money possessed by each person and the total number of car owners on the file
VAR MEN: **FILE OF** MALESTUDENT.

12.3 Assuming that the type SEX = (FEMALE, MALE), define a type STUDENT which combines both MALESTUDENT and FEMALESTUDENT, write a program to produce the same results as 12.2(a) and (b). The input will be from **VAR** CSSTUDENTS: **FILE OF** STUDENT.

13 Advanced Uses of Procedures and Functions

13.1 The Use of Procedures for Top-Down Design

The stepwise refinement technique described in chapter 3 eases the task of developing the solution to a problem. However, as the size of the problem tackled becomes larger, so do the number and complexity of the steps to be refined. This technique is only viable if the completely refined Pascal statements are sufficiently short to be understood as a whole (say, less than one page of program).

A problem may be reduced into sections by use of procedures. Since a procedure may contain declarations of other procedures (see chapter 6) further subdivision may be made, until the size of each section is suitable for refinement into Pascal.

Consider an imaginary problem which requires the initialisation of some data structures, the processing of some data and printing of results. Postponing consideration of any control constructs (repetition, choice, etc.), the problem might subdivide in the fashion shown in figure 13.1. Each box in the figure represents the *declaration* of a procedure/function or the body of a procedure/function or program. All of the procedures/functions used in each 'body' are given in the same column above it. Each procedure/function or program body of any complexity is refined using the procedures/functions shown in the column attached by a sloping line.

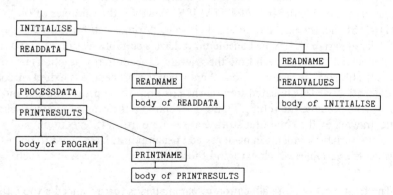

Figure 13.1   Subdivision of problem into procedures

At this stage it would be prudent to consider

(1) the position of the declarations of scalars and data structures
(2) the parameters to each of the procedures and
(3) the positioning of each of the procedure declarations in the 'tree'.

The statements in the body of each procedure may call any procedure/ function or use any variable higher up the tree. Thus declarations should be placed only as high up the tree as is compatible with their use. For example, the above tree would be improved, and the duplication of the READNAME procedure avoided, by moving this procedure to the top level.

Specification of the parameters of a procedure, any data structures used non-locally and any input/output all constitute a definition of the 'interface' of the procedure with the rest of the program. Only when this interface is understood, will it be productive to write the Pascal for the procedure.

The large example tackled in the next chapter uses this 'top-down' design technique.

13.2 A Further Discussion of Scope

Where the size of problem dictates heavy use of procedures, it may be found helpful to distinguish between the *existence* of a variable and its *accessibility*. In the imaginary problem above, for example, placement of the READNAME procedure at the top level of the program would illustrate this distinction. Within READNAME, called from INITIALISE, the rules of scope would prevent any access to the identifiers of INITIALISE. However, the variables of INITIALISE clearly exist and retain their value during a call for READNAME.

Declared variables may be considered to have a suitable section of computer store allocated to them, each time the relevant procedure (or function) is entered. This store is removed from them when the procedure is exited. A computer location is also allocated to note the position of the procedure call and hence make possible the return. Figure 13.2 shows a skeleton program, a schematic drawing of the computer storage at seven points in its execution, and a list of the variables which can be accessed at each point. Note the differences between the variables which exist and those which can be accessed at each point.

The treatment of store allocation to parameters is too advanced a topic to be covered here, but is similar to the treatment of variables declared within the procedure.

Example 13A

```
(* SKELETON PROGRAM TO DEMONSTRATE
   STORE ALLOCATION AND SCOPE OF VARIABLES *)
PROGRAM EX13A;
VAR I,J,K : INTEGER;
PROCEDURE A;
     VAR J,L,M : INTEGER;
     BEGIN
         .                 (* POINT 2 - CALL FROM PROGRAM *)
         .                 (* POINT 5 - CALL FROM PROCEDURE B *)
     END;
PROCEDURE B;
     VAR K,L,P : INTEGER;
     BEGIN
         .                 (* POINT 4 *)
         .
         A ;               (* CALL FOR PROCEDURE A *)
         .                 (* POINT 6 *)
         .
     END;
BEGIN
     .                     (* POINT 1 *)
     .
     A ;                   (* CALL FOR PROCEDURE A *)
     .                     (* POINT 3 *)
     .
     B ;                   (* CALL FOR PROCEDURE B *)
     .                     (* POINT 7 *)
     .
END.
```

ACCESSIBILITY (determined by scope)

STORE ALLOCATION	PROGRAM I J K	PROCEDURE A J L M	PROCEDURE B K L P
POINT 1 [I J K]	✓ ✓ ✓	X X X	X X X
POINT 2 [I J K][Return to POINT 3][J L M]	✓ X ✓	✓ ✓ ✓	X X X
POINT 3 [I J K]	✓ ✓ ✓	X X X	X X X
POINT 4 [I J K][Return to POINT 7][K L P]	✓ ✓ X	X X X	✓ ✓ ✓
POINT 5 [I J K][Return to POINT 7][K L P][Return to POINT 6][J L M]	✓ X ✓	✓ ✓ ✓	X X X
POINT 6 [I J K][Return to POINT 7][K L P]	✓ ✓ X	X X X	✓ ✓ ✓
POINT 7 [I J K]	✓ ✓ ✓	X X X	X X X

Figure 13.2 Existence and Accessibility of Variables of Example 13A

13.3   Procedure and Function Parameters

The discussion in chapter 6 concerning parameters was incomplete in two
respects. Firstly, as shown in the intervening chapters, variable and value parameters are not restricted to the four standard scalar types. However, structured
type parameters are usually variable parameters, since a value parameter implies
a local copy. In addition, file parameters *must* be specified as **VAR** and components of packed structures may *not* be used as actual variable parameters.

The second omission from previous discussion concerns the use of parameters
which are themselves procedures or functions—called 'procedure or function
parameters'. The complete syntax definition of parameter list is shown in
figure 13.3

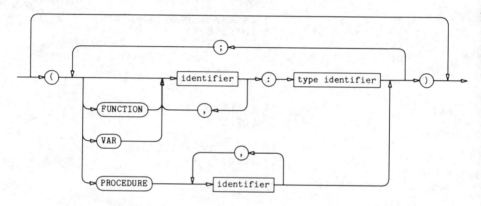

Figure 13.3

Where a section of program is to be written as a procedure or function, it is
possible that a procedure/function call may be included. It may be desirable to
vary the action of the procedure/function being written by making the enclosed
call a parameter. A call of the procedure being written must then specify an
actual procedure/function to be called, wherever the formal parameter is used.

Only the formal parameter name is given in the procedure heading, for a
procedure parameter. For a function parameter, the result type must also be
given. In both cases the calls for the formally named procedure or function,
within the procedure being declared, must have actual parameters consistent in
number and type with the parameters of the actual procedure/function given in
the calls of the new procedure.

Example 13B includes a procedure GRAPH, which outputs two star symbols
on each line of output and hence builds up a drawing of a graph of two functions.
The procedure is made more general in application, by making both of the
functions parameters. The formal function parameters F and G are both specified
to have REAL results and the calls for F and G each have one REAL parameter.
This is consistent with the declarations of the actual functions XSIN and XCOS.

Example 13B

```
(* DRAW A GRAPH OF TWO FUNCTIONS
   BY WRITING TWO STAR SYMBOLS ON EACH LINE *)
PROGRAM EX13B(OUTPUT);
FUNCTION XSIN(X :REAL) :REAL;
     BEGIN
     XSIN := X * SIN(X/10)
     END;
FUNCTION XCOS(X :REAL) :REAL;
     BEGIN
     XCOS := X * COS(X/100)
     END;
PROCEDURE GRAPH(FUNCTION F,G :REAL; MAX,MIN :REAL);
     CONST PAGEWIDTH = 80; (* CHARACTER POSITIONS *)
           LINELIMIT = 50; (* DEPTH OF PAGE *)
     VAR SCALE,X : REAL;
         I,A,B   : 0 .. PAGEWIDTH;
         LINENO : 0 .. LINELIMIT;
     PROCEDURE SWAP(VAR P,Q : INTEGER);
          VAR TEMP : INTEGER;
          BEGIN
          TEMP := P;
          P    := Q;
          Q    := TEMP
          END;
     BEGIN
     SCALE := PAGEWIDTH / (MAX-MIN);
     FOR LINENO := 0 TO LINELIMIT DO
          BEGIN
          X := LINENO;
          A := ROUND((F(X)-MIN) * SCALE);
          B := ROUND((G(X)-MIN) * SCALE);
          IF B < A THEN SWAP(A,B);
          FOR I := 1 TO A DO WRITE(' ');
          WRITE ('*');
          FOR I := A TO B-2 DO WRITE(' ');
          IF A <> B THEN WRITE('*');
          WRITELN
          END
     END;
BEGIN
GRAPH (XSIN, XCOS, 50, -50)
END.
```

Procedure/function actual parameters (for example, XSIN and XCOS) must have value parameters only (for example, X and Y). Further, on some computers, Pascal does not permit the use of standard procedures (for example, SIN, COS) as actual parameters.

13.4 Recursion

The scope of a procedure declaration includes its own body, and thus a procedure (or function) may be called from within itself. This would be the case if part of the action of a procedure was to perform another version of the same action. This is called 'recursion' and is used when writing 'recursive solutions' to problems. A very comprehensive discussion of this topic is given by Professor Wirth [1975*b*].

A solution is recursive if it is expressed in terms of the solution to simpler versions of the same problem and a specific statement about the simplest version of the problem. For example, consider the evaluation of the sum of all of the integers up to a number N.

   $1 + 2 + \ldots + N$

This could be re-expressed as

   $(1 + 2 + \ldots + N{-}1) + N$

while noting that the solution is trivial if $N = 1$. Thus program EX13C could be a solution to the problem.

Example 13C

```
(* SUM OF INTEGERS UP TO N
   SOLVED RECURSIVELY        *)
PROGRAM EX13C(INPUT,OUTPUT);
VAR NUMBER,TOTAL : INTEGER;
FUNCTION SUM(M : INTEGER) : INTEGER;
    BEGIN
    IF M = 1 THEN
        SUM := 1
    ELSE SUM := SUM(M - 1)  (*POINT 1*)  + M
    END;
BEGIN
READ(NUMBER);
TOTAL := SUM(NUMBER)  (*POINT 2*) ;
WRITELN('THE SUM OF INTEGERS UP TO', NUMBER:3,
        ' IS', TOTAL:6)
END.
```

When examining such solutions it should be noted that a new set of formal parameters and local variables is created each time the procedure/function is called. Figure 13.4 shows the state of the solution at each of the three calls and three returns from the function SUM.

In addition to explaining how recursion works within the computer, figure 13.4 demonstrates the cost involved in recursive solutions. This problem would be more efficiently solved by use of a simple repetition or, better, the formula

$$\text{SUM} = \frac{N(N + 1)}{2} \quad \text{or} \quad \text{count of numbers} * \text{average number}$$

The cost involved in recursion may often be avoided by use of repetition and a suitable data structure. However, it may be an elegant way of solving some problems. In example 13D the pocket calculator example of chapter 4 has been enhanced to cope with brackets.

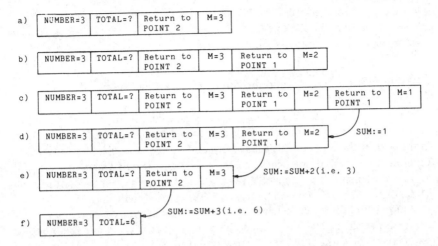

Figure 13.4   State of solution of program EX13C at six points

Example 13D

```
(* PROGRAM TO ACT AS A HAND CALCULATOR
   USING RECURSION TO DEAL WITH BRACKETS *)
PROGRAM EX13D(INPUT,OUTPUT);
VAR FINALANSWER : REAL;
FUNCTION EXPR : REAL;
    VAR OPERATOR      : CHAR;
        ANSWER,NEWNO  :REAL;
    BEGIN
    ANSWER := 0; OPERATOR := '+';
    REPEAT
        IF INPUT↑ = '(' THEN
            BEGIN
            GET(INPUT);
            NEWNO := EXPR    (* RECURSIVE CALL FOR
                                EXPR FUNCTION *)
            END
        ELSE READ (NEWNO);
        CASE OPERATOR OF
        '+': ANSWER := ANSWER + NEWNO;
        '-': ANSWER := ANSWER - NEWNO;
        '*': ANSWER := ANSWER * NEWNO;
        '/': ANSWER := ANSWER / NEWNO
        END;
        READ (OPERATOR)
    UNTIL OPERATOR IN [')' , '='] ;
    EXPR := ANSWER
    END;
BEGIN
FINALANSWER := EXPR;    (* OUTERMOST CALL OF
                           EXPR FUNCTION *)
WRITELN('ANSWER IS', FINALANSWER)
END.
```

A less usual form of recursion involves two procedures, A and B say. If the body of A contains a call for B *and* the body of B contains a call for A then the two procedures are 'mutually recursive' (see section 13.5).

13.5   Forward References and the Use of Library Procedures

A procedure (or function) may not normally be called from another procedure at the same or at a higher level, unless the procedure being called appears first in the text of the program. This may be inconvenient if some special textual ordering is desired for practical or aesthetic reasons. If two procedures are mutually recursive, it is impossible for both of them to appear before their calls. These difficulties are removed by use of a 'forward reference'.

A procedure (or function) may be forward referenced by separating its heading from the block. The heading may be given before any call and the block given later. The form of writing is shown in example 13E. Note that the parameters and function result type are not repeated at the body.

Example 13E

```
(* ARTIFICIAL EXAMPLE TO DEMONSTRATE
   STYLE OF WRITING FORWARD DECLARATIONS
   OF PROCEDURES AND FUNCTIONS            *)
PROGRAM EX13E;
PROCEDURE Q(X : REAL); FORWARD;
FUNCTION P( Y,Z : INTEGER) : REAL; FORWARD;
PROCEDURE R(I : INTEGER);
    VAR W : REAL;
    BEGIN
    .
    Q(3);
    .
    W := P(1,2);
    .
    END;
PROCEDURE Q;
    BEGIN
    .
    END;
FUNCTION P;
    BEGIN
    .
    END;
BEGIN

END.
```

A similar mechanism permits Pascal programs on most computers to call procedures which are not textually part of the program. This is the case if some procedures have been 'compiled' at an earlier time or if a 'procedure library' is to be used. These libraries are collections of useful procedures written by experts in the particular field of application. They are often comprehensive and sophisticated, and take much of the toil out of writing programs in areas where standard solutions and applications are well known.

External procedures (or functions) are declared by giving the heading and replacing the body of the procedure with the word EXTERN. Since many libraries are written in the language Fortran, the body may also be replaced by the word FORTRAN.

Example 13F uses a library of high-quality pen drawing procedures called GINO. The example draws rectangles at positions and sizes determined by the data read in. Note the four GINO procedures CN925, MOVTO2, LINBY2 and DEVEND which define the particular drawing device to be used, move to a given position, draw a line and complete the drawing, respectively. Local documentation should be consulted before making use of procedure libraries.

Example 13F

```
(* DRAW RECTANGLES ON PLOTTING DEVICE CN925
   USING GINO LIBRARY *)
PROGRAM EX13F(INPUT,OUTPUT);
VAR I,N : INTEGER;
    XPOSITION,YPOSITION,WIDTH,HEIGHT : REAL;
PROCEDURE CN925; FORTRAN;
PROCEDURE MOVTO2 (X,Y : REAL); FORTRAN;
PROCEDURE LINBY2 (X,Y : REAL); FORTRAN;
PROCEDURE DEVEND; FORTRAN;
BEGIN
CN925;
READ(N);
FOR I := 1 TO N DO
    BEGIN
    READ(XPOSITION,YPOSITION);
    MOVTO2(XPOSITION,YPOSITION);
    READ(WIDTH,HEIGHT);
    LINBY2(WIDTH,0.0);
    LINBY2(0.0,HEIGHT);
    LINBY2(-WIDTH,0.0);
    LINBY2(0.0,-HEIGHT)
    END;
DEVEND
END.
```

Exercises

13.1 Draw the state of the solution of program EX13D in the style of figure 13.4, assuming the data to be

$$1-((2*3)-(4*5))+(6/7)=$$

13.2 Write a boolean function whose result is TRUE if the value of a function parameter F is such that F(X) is positive at all of X = 0, 0.1, 0.2, . . . 1.0.

13.3 Investigate what libraries are available at your local installation. Do they include facilities for interactive graphics, numerical analysis, statistical and survey analysis, processing textual data and commercial data processing? Can you create your own library?

Problem

A problem which occupies some chess fanatics is how to place eight queens on a chess board, such that no queen can 'take' any other (that is, be on the same diagonal, horizontal or vertical). One solution is shown in figure 13.5. Note that there is only one queen in each column.

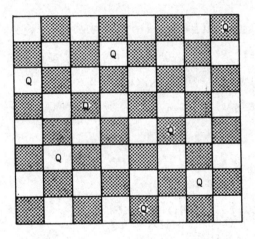

Figure 13.5

Algorithms have been published which solve this problem on a computer, but the reader will find it instructive to write his own Pascal solution. This might use a *recursive* procedure which chooses each of the eight positions to place the Ith queen and each time recurses to place the next, before removing the queen again. Whenever the eighth queen is placed, a solution has been found.

14 Dynamic Data Structures

14.1 Static and Dynamic Variables

The types of variable in Pascal programs have been classified (in chapter 7) as unstructured and structured. The structured types have been further subdivided into elementary structured types and advanced structured types. The variables themselves may also be divided into two groups, depending on the manner of their creation. Those introduced so far have the following characteristics.

(1) They are declared in **VAR** declarations which determine their types and their identifiers. These identifiers are used to refer to the variables.
(2) The variables declared in this way have a lifetime equal to the lifetime of the block in which they are declared. They are created on entry to the block and cease to exist when the computation exits from the block.

These are called 'static' variables.

Static variables may be used when the storage requirements of a program can be predicted at the time it is written. There are, however, many problems for which this prediction is not possible. Consider the following.

A Problem

The input data is a file of integers, which consists of several individual sequences of integers each terminated by zero (which is not a part of the sequence). The output is to be the same sequences in the same order, but with the numbers within each sequence in reverse order.

Sample input:	8	10	3	12	0	7	9	2	0	4	12	0
Sample output:	12	3	10	8	0	2	9	7	0	12	4	0

In this problem the lengths of the individual sequences are not known in advance, so that the variables needed to store the numbers must be created as the numbers are read in.

These are called 'dynamic' variables.

Dynamic variables are created on demand by obeying executable statements. Since they do not occur in variable declarations, dynamic variables cannot be referenced directly by identifiers. Instead, associated with each dynamic variable of the type T there is a value, of the type ↑T (pronounced 'pointer-to-T'), which is used to access the corresponding dynamic variable. This value is usually the store address of the newly created variable, permitting efficient access to the dynamic variable (see figure 14.1).

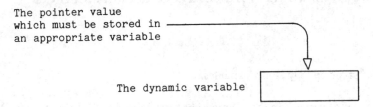

Figure 14.1

A dynamic variable will exist until either it is explicitly destroyed (see section 14.4) or the computation ceases.

Since dynamic variables may be of any type T, it is possible to create record variables dynamically. If these records contain one or more fields of the type ↑T then complex structures may be created, by linking the records together (see figure 14.2)

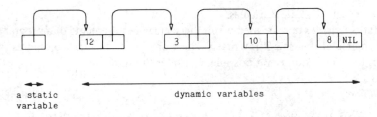

Figure 14.2   The first sequence stored in dynamic variables

The creation and manipulation of these structures is a very important topic in computer science and merits more time than can be afforded in this introductory text. However, an outline will be given of the applications for which dynamic variables and their pointers are often used.

Dynamic variables may be formed into chains to create linear lists, which can be used to model sequences. Orthogonally linked linear lists may be used to model very large but sparsely filled matrices. This is an example of an important use of dynamic variables, namely, the modelling of elementary data structures whose large cardinality makes use of the appropriate elementary data structure prohibitively expensive. It is, of course, possible to model these large cardinality data structures without having to resort to pointers.

The most common use of dynamic variables is the modelling of dynamic data structures. The dynamic data structures are all members of the class of advanced data structures. In addition to the property of having an infinite cardinality, they have the property that their *structure* may change dynamically during the course of the computation. Trees and graphs are examples of such data structures.

14.2 The Creation of Dynamic Variables

Dynamic variables are created in Pascal programs by calling the standard procedure NEW. This procedure has two forms. In the simpler case, NEW(P), it takes one parameter, which is a pointer variable of type ↑T. The action of the procedure is simple. It creates a dynamic variable of type T by allocating space for it from an area of Pascal storage called, appropriately, the 'heap'. It also assigns to the parameter a value of the type ↑T, so that the dynamic variable may be accessed. If there is insufficient space on the heap to create the dynamic variable, the program fails during execution and an appropriate† message is output. For example, the following declarations are suitable for generating the list of figure 14.2.

```
TYPE PTR  = ↑ITEM;
     ITEM = RECORD
              VAL  : INTEGER;
              NEXT : PTR
            END;
VAR  P,LIST  : PTR;
     X       : INTEGER;
     INTFILE : FILE OF INTEGER;
```

The list may be created thus

```
(* INITIALISE THE LIST *)
READ(INTFILE,X);
WHILE X <> 0 DO
  BEGIN
  NEW(P);
  (* RECORD THE INTEGER *)
  (* AND LINK INTO *)
  (* THE LIST *)
  READ(INTFILE,X)
  END;
```

Notes (a) The syntax diagram of a pointer type is
(b) The type identifier in a pointer type declaration may refer forwards to an as yet undeclared identifier. This is the *only* example of the use of an identifier prior to its declaration in Pascal.
(c) A pointer variable may point to dynamic variables of one type only.

† In many Pascal implementations the storage areas used for the heap and the stack (on which all the explicitly declared variables reside) advance towards each other. This means that heap overflow and stack overflow produce similar conditions. Even though it is possible to distinguish between these two conditions, the same error message—RUN TIME STACK OVERFLOW—is often produced in both cases.

The NEW procedure is the only mechanism provided in Pascal for creating values of pointer types. Thus it is not possible to create a pointer value which refers to an explicitly declared (static) variable. This is *not* a deficiency in Pascal, but a deliberate decision which improves the security, efficiency and readability of Pascal programs.

The second form of the procedure NEW may only be used when creating record variables which have variants. If created with the simpler form of NEW, the resulting variable is able to hold values of any of the variants. In many instances it is known, when it is being created, that a dynamic variable will only assume values of one particular variant. This variant may require less storage than the largest variant. In this case it is possible to use the second form of the procedure NEW, which is

$$NEW(P, t1, \ldots, tn)$$

where P is a pointer variable as before. The values t1 to tn are a series of tag field values and identify the particular variant required, for example

NEW(P, STUDENT, TRUE).

Notes (a) The tag field values t1 to tn must all be *constants*.
(b) The tag field values must be listed contiguously and in the order of their declaration. Trailing values may be omitted.
(c) The use of this form of the NEW procedure does *not* cause the tag field values supplied to be assigned to their respective tag fields.

Caution

The second form of the NEW procedure provides a means of optimising the use of the heap in some applications. It may be an unsafe optimisation. Many implementations of Pascal impose restrictions on the use of dynamic variables created in this way—restrictions which they do not subsequently check! For example, assignment to an entire dynamic variable is not allowed. For this reason the second form of NEW should be used with care by the experienced programmer and not at all by the beginner!

14.3 Using Pointers

In Pascal, pointers may be used in the following ways. They may be
   assigned
   passed as parameters
   tested for equality or inequality, or
   used to access dynamic variables.
Every pointer type has a set of values which includes the value **NIL**. This does not point to a dynamic variable and may be assigned to pointer variables to indicate the absence of a usable pointer value. It was used in figure 14.2 to indicate the end of the list.

The accessing of dynamic variables is best described by examples. Assuming the declarations from section 14.2, P and LIST are static variables which may point to (reference) dynamic variables of type ITEM. The identifiers P and LIST will always mean the static variables, so that

    P := LIST;

causes P to contain the same pointer value as LIST. The notation P↑ means 'the dynamic variable referenced by P'. So P↑ is of the type ITEM. To assign the value of the dynamic variable referenced by LIST to that referenced by P

    P↑ := LIST↑ ;

Since P↑ is of the type ITEM, a field selector may be applied, as in

    P↑.VAL := X;

A complete solution to the resequencing problem is now possible.

Example 14A

```
PROGRAM EX14A(OUTPUT,INTFILE,NEWFILE);
TYPE PTR  = ↑ITEM;
     ITEM = RECORD
                VAL  : INTEGER;
                NEXT : PTR
            END;
VAR X : INTEGER;
    P,LIST : PTR;
    INTFILE,NEWFILE : FILE OF INTEGER;
BEGIN
RESET(INTFILE); REWRITE(NEWFILE);
WHILE NOT EOF(INTFILE) DO
  BEGIN
  (* READ IN A SEQUENCE *)
  LIST := NIL; (* INITIALISE THE LIST *)
  READ(INTFILE,X);
  WHILE X <> 0 DO
    BEGIN
    NEW(P);
    P↑.VAL := X;      (* RECORD THE INTEGER *)
    P↑.NEXT := LIST; (* AND LINK INTO *)
    LIST := P;        (* THE LIST *)
    READ(INTFILE,X)
    END;
  (* OUTPUT THE SEQUENCE IN REVERSE *)
  P := LIST;
  WHILE P <> NIL DO
    BEGIN
    WRITE(NEWFILE,P↑.VAL);
    P := P↑.NEXT   (* ADVANCE DOWN THE CHAIN *)
    END;
  WRITE(NEWFILE,0)
  END
END.
```

14.4   Re-using Dynamically Allocated Storage

Program EX14A has a very obvious deficiency. No attempt has been made to re-use unwanted dynamic variables. As a result of this, the program needs a heap large enough to store the whole input file and all the pointers. Once a sequence has been output the space it occupied could be recovered for future use. If this were done, the heap need only be big enough to hold the longest sequence.

There are several different ways of dealing with this problem.

14.4.1   Using DISPOSE

The procedure DISPOSE is exactly the reverse of NEW. It has a single parameter, a pointer variable, which points to an unwanted dynamic variable. Its action is to recover the space for future use and assign the value NIL to its parameter. There is a second form of DISPOSE which has tag field parameters. This form *must* be used to dispose any unwanted dynamic variables created using the second form of NEW. The tag field parameters must be *identical* to the ones used when the variable was created.

Warnings

(1) Some early Pascal implementations provided a DISPOSE procedure which merely assigned NIL to its parameter.
(2) It is the programmer's responsibility to ensure that the variables disposed are really unwanted and that no additional references to them exist. Some implementations will fault any attempt to reference a disposed dynamic variable.

Program EX14A can now be modified to use DISPOSE. An additional variable, for example, EXP, of type PTR will be needed. The statement P := P↑.NEXT is simply replaced by

```
EXP := P;        (* NOTE POINTER VALUE OF UNWANTED VARIABLE *)
P := P↑.NEXT;
DISPOSE(EXP);    (* RECOVER STORE FROM UNWANTED VARIABLE *)
```

14.4.2   Using MARK and RELEASE

Although the DISPOSE procedure is the standard mechanism for returning unwanted dynamic variables, some implementations based on the Pascal-P compiler provide MARK and RELEASE. Both these procedures require a pointer variable as a parameter. When MARK is called, it records the current state of the heap in the parameter provided. This parameter must not be altered until the corresponding release. All dynamic variables created since the heap was marked may be returned simultaneously by calling RELEASE with the same parameter as a MARK. This method is only of use in a limited number of applications. By using several different variables as parameters, the marking and releasing effects may be nested.

To modify program EX14A to use MARK and RELEASE is straightforward. An additional pointer variable (of any type) is needed to hold the mark information, for example, EXP of type ↑INTEGER. The heap is marked before LIST is initialised using MARK(EXP), and is released before the statement WRITE (NEWFILE, 0) using RELEASE(EXP).

Warnings

(1) It is the programmer's responsibility to ensure that the variables released are really unwanted. Any references to these variables from static variables or non-released dynamic variables will remain unchanged. Any attempt to use these references will cause chaos!

(2) MARK and RELEASE should not be used in the same program as DISPOSE.

14.4.3 Using a Free-list

If a Pascal implementation does not provide any suitable procedures for returning dynamic variables, it is always possible to program a free-list scheme. Using this scheme all unwanted variables are added to a list. The procedure NEW is then only called if this list becomes empty. This scheme has two disadvantages when compared with the predefined procedures already described.

(1) A separate free-list must be maintained for every type of dynamic variable in use.

(2) The space created by returning variables using the predefined procedures may be used for other purposes. In some implementations, for example, it could be used for static variables.

14.5 The London Underground Problem

The problem is simply this: given a description of the London Underground network and the cost (in some units) of travel between all adjacent points in the network, find either (1) the shortest route from a given source to a given destination, or (2) the shortest route from a given source to all destinations. In the second case the routes would be printed on request.

This problem has several interesting qualities. It is a real-life problem and consequently there are many irregularities and pecularities; nevertheless, an existing published algorithm may be used to solve it provided a suitable data structure can be found.

Representing the London Underground on the Input File

Consider a simple station on the Underground. For the purposes of this problem it consists of three interconnected points (NODES)—see figure 14.3.

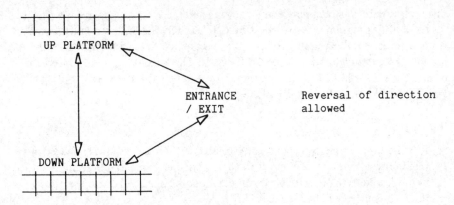

Figure 14.3

The crux of the matter is that changing directions on the same line will require changing trains and must be controlled in the model which the data structure creates. If walking between the up and down platforms is prohibited one can always leave the station and buy another ticket. In this case the model would be as shown in figure 14.4.

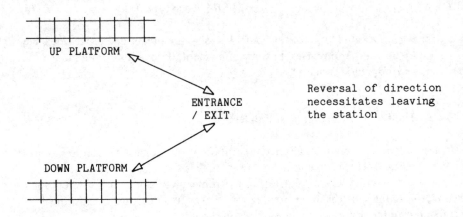

Figure 14.4

A station which is an interchange between two or more lines, or which is followed by a fork in the Underground lines, can be dealt with in a similar manner.

Each node will be given a name, which will, if necessary, indicate the choice of line and direction of travel, as well as the name of the station.

The network will be represented on the input as a sequence of single direction connections with an associated cost. The format will be

NAME1   NAME2   COST

which indicates that it is possible to go from node NAME1 to node NAME2 at
the specified cost. The cost is likely to be a measure of the time taken. When
described in this way, the London Underground will consist of approximately
1000 nodes and 4000 interconnections.

Designing the Algorithm and Data Structures

There are many approaches to the problem of designing algorithms and data
structures in computer programming. First one should see if any well-known
algorithms may be used. In this instance the Underground network may be
viewed as a directed graph, so graph-processing algorithms may be useful. One
such is due to Dijkstra [Aho *et al.*, 1974, 207-9]. This algorithm calculates the
minimum cost routes between one source and all destinations subject to certain
constraints.

Given that the term 'fixed' means that a quantity 'total cost' cannot be reduced and is therefore to be left unchanged, then, in general terms, Dijkstra's
algorithm can be stated as follows.

Step 1   Set to zero the total cost to get to the source. Fix this total cost.
Step 2   Initialise the total costs of all the destinations thus
             to MAXINT if not connected directly to the source
             to the cost of the route from the source if directly connected.
Step 3   While there are some destinations without a fixed total cost, per-
             form steps 4 through 6.
Step 4   Choose a destination which has the smallest cost, which has not yet
             been fixed. Call this destination W.
Step 5   Fix the total cost of W.
Step 6   Examine all destinations which can be reached directly from W. If
             travel from W (whose minimum total cost is known) and subse-
             quent travel to the destination produces a lower total cost than
             the best for that destination, then adjust the total cost accordingly.

Unfortunately, the obvious encoding of this algorithm requires an n x n matrix,
where n is 1000 (approximately), and variables of the type **SET OF** 0 . . 1000.
Of course, this does not necessarily mean that the algorithm cannot be used. An
examination of the above algorithm reveals that the data structure need not be
accessed randomly. Steps 3 and 4 involve the examination of all the nodes sequentially. Step 6 requires the examination of all the nodes adjacent to a
selected node. This suggests the following

```
TYPE NODE = RECORD
            NAME       : NODENAME;
            TOTALCOST  : INTEGER;
            COSTFIXED  : BOOLEAN;
            (* DETAILS OF ADJACENT NODES *)
            END;
```

The number of adjacent nodes varies greatly from node to node. The sequential accessing of this information and a desire to minimise storage space suggests a linked list of destinations.

```
TYPE PDEST        = ↑DESTINATION;
     PNODE        = ↑NODE;
     DESTINATION = RECORD
                       DEST : PNODE;
                       NEXT : PDEST;
                       COST : INTEGER
                   END;
```

The number of nodes is an unknown quantity so they too should be in a linked list. This needs an additional field in the NODE, for example,
REST : PNODE.

There is now one remaining difficulty. Dijkstra's algorithm computes the cost of the shortest route, but does not give an indication of the route itself. A minor modification to steps 2 and 6 will rectify this. This produces the type declarations shown in example 14B (for convenience all the non-procedural declarations are given).

Example 14B

```
PROGRAM EX14B(INPUT,OUTPUT,UNDATA);
CONST NAMELENGTH = 30;
TYPE NODENAME = PACKED ARRAY[1..NAMELENGTH] OF CHAR;
     PNODE = ↑NODE;
     PDEST = ↑DESTINATION;
     MESSAGE = PACKED ARRAY[1..20] OF CHAR;
     POSINT = 0 .. MAXINT;
     NODE =    PACKED RECORD
                   NAME :      NODENAME;
                   COSTFIXED : BOOLEAN;
                   TOTALCOST : POSINT;
                   MINTOHERE : PNODE;
                   NEXT :      PDEST;
                   REST :      PNODE
               END;
     DESTINATION = PACKED RECORD
                       DEST : PNODE;
                       NEXT : PDEST;
                       COST : POSINT
                   END;
VAR NOOFNODES : INTEGER;
    S1,S2,SENTINEL,FIRSTNODE : PNODE;
    UNDATA : TEXT;
    CH : CHAR;
```

The main program for case (2) in the problem specification can be broken down as follows.

```
BEGIN (* MAIN PROGRAM *)
CREATEUNDERGROUND;
ENQUIRE(' WHERE ARE YOU NOW   ',S1);
CALCULATECOSTS(S1);
(* PROCESS ENQUIRIES *)
REPEAT
  ENQUIRE(' WHERE ARE YOU GOING',S2);
  PRINTROUTE(S2);
  WRITELN(' ANY MORE');
  READLN; READ(CH)
UNTIL CH <> 'Y'
END.
```

The CREATEUNDERGROUND procedure may be broken down into a few
steps in a similar manner.

```
PROCEDURE CREATEUNDERGROUND;
  VAR NAME1,NAME2 : NODENAME;
      S1,S2 : PNODE;
      COST : POSINT;
  BEGIN
  NEW(SENTINEL); FIRSTNODE := SENTINEL;
  NOOFNODES := 0;
  RESET(UNDATA);
  WHILE NOT EOF(UNDATA) DO
    BEGIN
    READNAME(UNDATA,NAME1);READNAME(UNDATA,NAME2);
    READLN(UNDATA,COST);
    LOOKUPNAME(NAME1,S1,TRUE); LOOKUPNAME(NAME2,S2,TRUE);
    LINKNODES(S1,S2,COST)
    END
  END; (* OF CREATEUNDERGROUND *)
```

There is a point of interest here—a sentinel node is created which is always at
the end of the list of nodes. This greatly simplifies the terminating condition of
the search loop in the LOOKUPNAME procedure.

```
PROCEDURE LOOKUPNAME(N : NODENAME;VAR S : PNODE; CREATE : BOOLEAN);
  VAR P : PNODE;
  BEGIN
  SENTINEL↑.NAME := N; P := FIRSTNODE;
  WHILE P↑.NAME <> N DO P := P↑.REST;
  IF P <> SENTINEL THEN S := P (* ALREADY EXISTS *)
  ELSE IF NOT CREATE THEN S := NIL (* NOT THERE *)
      ELSE
        BEGIN
        NEW(SENTINEL);
        WITH P↑ DO
          BEGIN
          COSTFIXED := FALSE; TOTALCOST := MAXINT;
          NEXT := NIL;
          REST := SENTINEL; NOOFNODES := NOOFNODES + 1;
          MINTOHERE := NIL (* NOT STRICTLY NECESSARY *)
          END;
        S := P
        END
  END; (* OF LOOKUPNAME *)
```

The LOOKUPNAME procedure can be used in two ways. This is determined by the CREATE parameter. If this is TRUE then a node will be created if the search fails.

The only other procedure of interest is the CALCULATECOSTS procedure. This is simply a Pascal encoding of the algorithm described already, with steps 2 and 6 amended. In this encoding, frequent use has been made of the **WITH** statement. In particular, note the occurrences of

WITH P↑, DEST↑ **DO**

To appreciate the improvement in clarity and efficiency that these provide, the reader is urged to re-code this procedure without using any **WITH** statements.

```
PROCEDURE CALCULATECOSTS(SOURCE : PNODE);
  VAR COUNT,MAX : POSINT;
      P : PDEST;
      S,W : PNODE;
  BEGIN
  COUNT := 1;
  (* STEP 1 *)
  WITH SOURCE↑ DO
    BEGIN
    TOTALCOST := 0;COSTFIXED := TRUE; P := NEXT
    END;
  (* STEP 2 *)
  WHILE P <> NIL DO
    BEGIN
    WITH P↑,DEST↑ DO
      BEGIN
      TOTALCOST := COST; MINTOHERE := SOURCE
      END;
    P := P↑.NEXT
    END;
  (* STEP 3 *)
  WHILE COUNT <> NOOFNODES DO
    BEGIN
    (* STEP 4 *)
    S := FIRSTNODE; MAX := MAXINT;
    WHILE S <> SENTINEL DO
      BEGIN
      WITH S↑ DO
        BEGIN
        IF NOT COSTFIXED THEN
          IF TOTALCOST < MAX THEN
            BEGIN
            MAX := TOTALCOST; W := S
            END
        END;
        S := S↑.REST
      END;
```

```
(* STEP 5 *)
W↑.COSTFIXED := TRUE; COUNT := COUNT + 1;
(* STEP 6 *)
P := W↑.NEXT;
WHILE P <> NIL DO
  BEGIN
  WITH P↑,DEST↑ DO
    BEGIN
    IF NOT COSTFIXED THEN
      IF COST + MAX < TOTALCOST THEN
        BEGIN
        TOTALCOST := COST + MAX; MINTOHERE := W
        END
    END;
    P := P↑.NEXT
  END (* OF STEP 6 *)
  END (* OF STEP 3 *)
END; (* OF CALCULATE COSTS *)
```

If the program has only to solve the originally specified case (1), then the destination (TARGET) should be known before the costs are calculated. A gain in efficiency may then be achieved by deleting all references to COUNT and replacing

```
WHILE COUNT <> NOOFNODES DO
```

by

```
WHILE NOT TARGET↑.COSTFIXED DO
```

The remaining procedures are included for completeness. For simplicity the **PRINTROUTE** procedure outputs the route in reverse. This can easily be altered (exercise 14.3).

```
PROCEDURE READNAME(VAR F : TEXT;VAR N : NODENAME);
  VAR CH : CHAR;
      I : 1..72;
  BEGIN
  N := '
  WHILE F↑ = ' ' DO GET(F);
  I := 1;
  WHILE F↑ <> ' ' DO
    BEGIN
    READ(F,CH);
    IF I <= NAMELENGTH THEN
      BEGIN
      N[I] := CH ; I := I + 1
      END
    END
  END; (* OF READNAME *)
```

```
PROCEDURE LINKNODES(S1,S2 : PNODE; C : POSINT);
   VAR P : PDEST;
   BEGIN
   NEW(P);
   WITH P↑ DO
      BEGIN
      NEXT := S1↑.NEXT; DEST := S2; COST := C; S1↑.NEXT := P
      END
   END; (* OF LINKNODES *)
PROCEDURE PRINTROUTE(DEST : PNODE);
   VAR P : PNODE;
   BEGIN
   WRITELN(' THE BEST ROUTE IS ');
   P := DEST;
   WHILE P <> NIL DO
      BEGIN
      WRITELN(P↑.NAME);
      P := P↑.MINTOHERE
      END
   END; (* OF PRINTROUTE *)
PROCEDURE ENQUIRE(MESS : MESSAGE; VAR ST : PNODE);
   VAR S     : PNODE;
       NAME : NODENAME;
   BEGIN
   REPEAT
      WRITELN(MESS);
      READNAME(INPUT,NAME);
      LOOKUPNAME(NAME,S,FALSE)
   UNTIL S <> NIL;
   ST := S
   END; (* OF ENQUIRE *)
```

Exercises

14.1 The input file which describes the London Underground is very long.
During the creation of the file, errors may have been introduced which mean
that certain nodes are not connected properly. Modify the CALCULATECOSTS
procedure, in a simple way, to detect such a situation when it occurs and print
out a suitable message.

14.2 Modify the LOOKUPNAME procedure in program EX14B, so that the
station names are held in alphabetical order. Will this change the efficiency of
the program?

14.3 Modify the PRINTROUTE procedure of program EX14B to print the
route in the correct order. The program must be able to function without change.

14.4 Choose a data structure suitable for representing a set whose base type has a large cardinality, for example, **SET OF** 0 .. MAXINT. You may assume that the sets will not have many members. Show how one or more of the Pascal set operators may be programmed using this data structure.

Problems

14.1 Write a set of procedures which will read, write, add and multiply positive integers of unlimited precision.

14.2 Write a program which will model a world governed by the laws of Conway's 'Game of Life' (see *Scientific American*, Oct. 1970, Feb. 1971). It is clearly impossible to simulate an infinite world on a finite computer, so some limitations must be placed on the size of the world, the size of the population, or both. Since some simulations last for many moves it is *essential* that the program be efficient. You may limit your considerations to the simulation of worlds with no more than 10 000 cells and populations of less than 500 organisms.

14.3 The soccer results that appear in the newspapers are in two parts: (1) the results of the matches, (2) the new state of the league table, which takes into account the results of the matches. Write a program which will accept as data
   (a) the results of the matches
   (b) the old league table
to produce as output the new league table formed by incorporating the results of the matches played.
   The results will be presented to the program as a text file in the form

   team name   no. of goals   team name   no. of goals   end of line

   etc.

For example

   Liverpool   0   Everton   1

   Man. City   0   Man. Utd   4

The first team is the 'home' team, the second the 'away' team. The league tables contain the following information relating to each team: team name, number of games played, number of points accumulated. The following details are also kept of each team's performance at home and away: number of games won, drawn and lost; total number of goals scored for; total number of goals scored against. The number of points awarded to a team for each game are

   2 if won, 1 if drawn and 0 if lost

The old and new league tables will be of type

FILE OF LTENTRY

where LTENTRY has been defined thus

```
TYPE LOCALITY = (HOME,AWAY);
     POSINT   = 0 .. MAXINT;
     LTENTRY  = RECORD
                TEAM    : ALFA;
                PLAYED  : POSINT;
                POINTS  : POSINT;
                DETAILS : ARRAY [LOCALITY] OF
                          RECORD
                          WON          : POSINT;
                          DRAWN        : POSINT;
                          LOST         : POSINT;
                          GOALSFOR     : POSINT;
                          GOALSAGAINST : POSINT
                          END
            END;
```

The ordering of the old and new league tables is immaterial.

Appendix I Pascal Syntax Diagrams

identifier

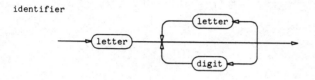

unsigned integer

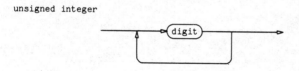

unsigned number

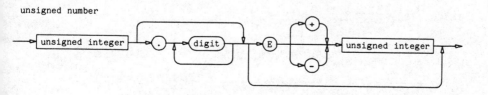

unsigned constant

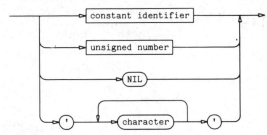

constant

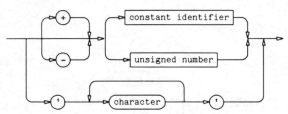

simple type

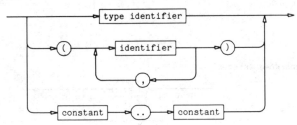

type

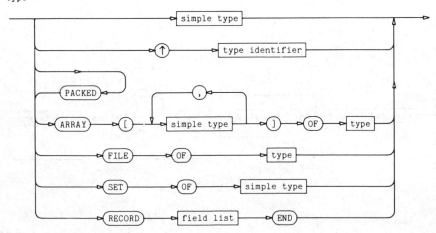

field list

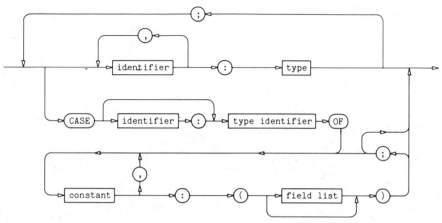

variable

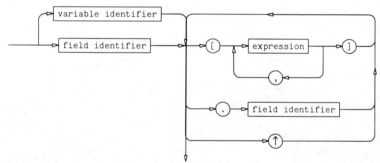

factor

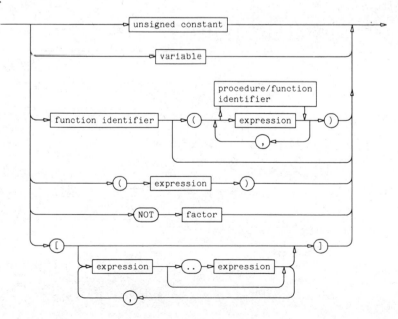

term

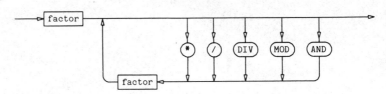

simple expression

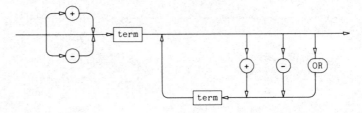

expression

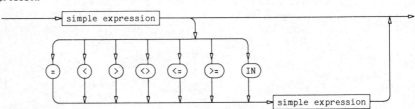

parameter list

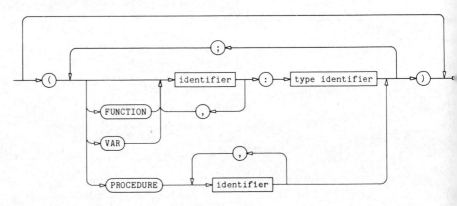

statement

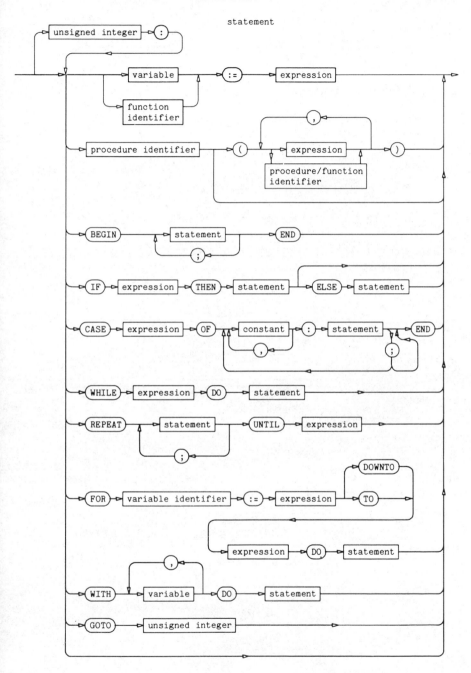

block

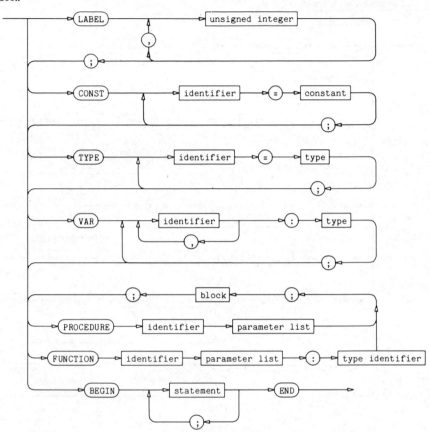

program

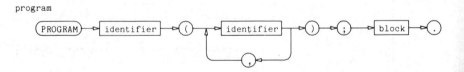

Appendix II   List of Pascal Delimiter Words

AND	NIL
ARRAY	NOT
BEGIN	OF
CASE	OR
CONST	PACKED
DIV	PROCEDURE
DO	PROGRAM
DOWNTO	RECORD
ELSE	REPEAT
END	SET
FILE	THEN
FOR	TO
FUNCTION	TYPE
GOTO	UNTIL
IF	VAR
IN	WHILE
LABEL	WITH
MOD	

Appendix III   Answers to Exercises and Schema for Selected Problems

Chapter 1

shopping list item

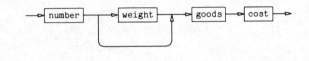

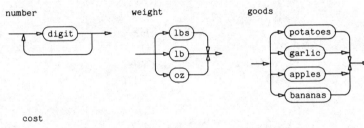

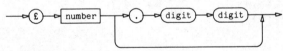

Chapter 2

2.1

legal: X,X1,X1X,TEMPERATURE,ANTIDISESTABLISHMENTARIANISM
illegal: 1X—starts with digit
            JOHN BROWN—space
            RE-ACTIVATE— –
            TEMPERATE—possibly legal but inadvisable as first eight characters
                            same as TEMPERATURE
            X(3)—brackets
            BEGIN, CASE—both are delimiters

2.2

line 1   ; missing
line 2   J should be declared REAL as 3.4 is real.

                    K should be declared
line 6   ; missing
line 7   left side of assignment must be a variable
line 9   period missing

2.3 Lay out neatly—use meaningful identifiers—use comments—use
CONSTants—make output readable.

```
(* PROGRAM TO PRINT THE SUM OF TWO INTEGERS *)
PROGRAM EX2A(INPUT,,OUTPUT);.
VAR NUMBER1,NUMBER2,SUM : INTEGER;
BEGIN
READ(NUMBER1,NUMBER2);
SUM := NUMBER1 + NUMBER2;
WRITELN ('THE TOTAL IS', SUM)
END.
```

Chapter 3

3.1(a)
```
IF PENCE = 0 THEN
        WRITELN('ZERO')
ELSE WRITELN('NON ZERO')
```

(b)
```
IF I <= 200 THEN
        T := 0
ELSE IF I <= 400 THEN
            T := (I-200) * 0.3
        ELSE IF I <= 5000 THEN
                    T := 200*0.3 + (I-400)*0.4
                ELSE T := 200*0.3 + (I-400)*0.5
```

3.2
```
MAX := 0;
REPEAT
        READ(NUM);
        IF NUM > MAX THEN MAX := NUM
UNTIL NUM = 0;
WRITELN('BIGGEST IS', MAX)
```

3.3
```
FOR I := 1 TO 200 DO
        BEGIN
        READ(ANIMAL);
        CASE ANIMAL OF
         1:  WRITELN('LION');
         2:  WRITELN('TIGER');
         3:  WRITELN('FLY');
             .
             .
             .
        END (* OF CASE *)
        END
```

Problem 3.2

```
(* INITIALISE COUNT TO 3 *)
FOR M := 5 TO 500 DO
     BEGIN
     (* DETERMINE IF M IS PRIME
        BY DIVIDING BY ALL NUMBERS, N
        STARTING AT M - 1 AND UNTIL
        M DIVIDES EXACTLY BY N          *)
     IF N = 1 THEN (* INCREMENT COUNT *)
     END;
(* PRINT ANSWER *)
```

Chapter 4

4.1(a) A * SQR(X) + B * X + C
(b) 0.5 * (X * Y + Z / (3 * X))
(c) SQRT(SQR(A) + SQR(B))

4.2(a) 1.0E−7
(b) 6.55260034E4
(c) −7.5E−1

4.3(a) 0.1666667   **(b)** 1.25   **(c)** 5   **(d)** 3   **(e)** 5

4.4(a) I **MOD** J = 0
(b) **NOT** (ODD(M))
(c) (ABS(Y)<1) **OR** (ABS(Y)>2)

4.5   P **AND** (X >= Y) **OR** (I<>J)

Chapter 5

5.1
```
FOR I := 1 TO 20 DO
     BEGIN
     WHILE NOT EOLN DO
          BEGIN
          READ(CH);
          IF (CH = 'A') OR (CH = 'E') OR (CH = 'I')
          OR (CH = 'O') OR (CH = 'U') THEN
               WRITE(CH)
          END;
     READLN
     END
```

5.2

EMPL NO.	INCOME	EXPENSES	DEPENDENTS	EMPLTYPE	TAX
I : 8	R:9:2	R:9:2	' ':10 I:1	' ':8 I:1	R:8:2

where I = INTEGER and R = REAL

Chapter 6

6.1 line 4   — **PROCEDURE** DRAWALINE(CH : CHAR);
        line 9   — ʼ WRITE(CH);
after   line 14   — DRAWALINE ('+');
after   lines 16, 19 — DRAWALINE ('–');

6.2(a) line 2   — **FUNCTION** TOTAL : INTEGER;
          line 10 — TOTAL := SUM
          indent body and change . to ;

(b) line 2   — **FUNCTION** MAXPOWER(A,B:REAL):INTEGER;
        line 3   — delete A,B,
        line 6   — delete
        line 13 — MAXPOWER := POWER
        indent body and change . to ;

(c) line 2   — **FUNCTION** AV(N : INTEGER) : REAL;
        line 3   — delete , N
        line 6   — delete READ(N);
        line 13 — AV := AVERAGE
        indent body and change . to ;

6.3

```
(* LENGTHS ARITHMETIC *)
PROGRAM EX6E(INPUT,OUTPUT);
VAR A,B,C,D,TOTAL : INTEGER;
PROCEDURE CONVERT
          (VAR M,Y,F,I : INTEGER;
                    INS : INTEGER);
     BEGIN
     M := INS DIV (1760*36);           all of the
     INS := INS MOD (1760*36);         identifiers
     Y := INS DIV 36;                  of CONVERT
     INS := INS MOD 36;                and PROGRAM
     F := INS DIV 12;
     I := INS MOD 12
     END;
FUNCTION INCHES
          (M,Y,F,I : INTEGER) : INTEGER;
     BEGIN                             all of the
     INCHES :=                         identifiers
     (((M*1760) + Y)*3 + F)*12 + I      of INCHES
     END;                              and PROGRAM
BEGIN
READ(A,B,C,D);
TOTAL := INCHES(A,B,C,D);
READ(A,B,C,D);
TOTAL := TOTAL + INCHES(A,B,C,D);      all of the
CONVERT(A,B,C,D,TOTAL);                identifiers
WRITELN('SUM IS', TOTAL,               of PROGRAM
 ' INCHES - I.E.');
WRITELN(A:4, ' MILES,',
        B:4, ' YARDS,',
        C:1, ' FEET AND',
        D:2, ' INCHES')
END.
```

Chapter 7

7.1 Implementation dependent.

7.2 Implementation dependent.

7.3 In the following examples the specified variables could have been declared as indicated.

3B   POWER : 0. .MAXINT;

3E   A,B:0. .MAXINT;

3G   POSCOUNT,NEGCOUNT : 0. .MAXINT;

3H   POSITIVESUM : 0. .MAXINT;
        NEGATIVESUM : −MAXINT. .0;
        COUNT : 0. .MAXINT;

3I   DAYNO : 1. .7;

3L   EMPLTYPE : 1. .3;
        DEPENDENTS : 0. .MAXINT;

5B   CENTEMP : 0. .99;

6A   I : 1. .LENGTH;

6D   INS and NUMBER : 0. .MAXINT
        M and A : 0. . MAXINT
        Y and B : 0. .1760
        F and C : 0. .2
        I and D : 0. .11

6E   Similar to 6D

6F   I : 1. .WIDTH;

Chapter 8

8.1

```
PROGRAM LINECOUNT(F,OUTPUT);
VAR F : TEXT;
    LINECOUNT : 0..MAXINT;
BEGIN
RESET(F);
LINECOUNT := 0;
WHILE NOT EOF(F) DO
  BEGIN
  READLN(F);
  LINECOUNT := LINECOUNT + 1
  END;
WRITELN(LINECOUNT)
END.
```

8.2

```
PROGRAM LINESTATS(F,OUTPUT);
VAR F : TEXT;
    MINIMUM,MAXIMUM,COUNT,TOTAL,LINECOUNT : 0..MAXINT;
BEGIN
RESET(F);
MINIMUM := MAXINT; MAXIMUM := 0; TOTAL := 0; LINECOUNT := 0;
WHILE NOT EOF(F) DO
  BEGIN
  COUNT := 0;
  WHILE NOT EOLN(F) DO
    BEGIN
    GET(F);
    COUNT := COUNT + 1
    END;
  READLN(F);
  IF COUNT < MINIMUM THEN MINIMUM := COUNT;
  IF COUNT > MAXIMUM THEN MAXIMUM := COUNT;
  TOTAL := TOTAL + COUNT;
  LINECOUNT := LINECOUNT + 1
  END;
IF LINECOUNT <> 0 THEN WRITELN(MINIMUM,MAXIMUM,TOTAL/LINECOUN
ELSE WRITELN(' EMPTY FILE ')
END.
```

8.3

```
PROGRAM MERGE(F,G,OUT,OUTPUT);
VAR CONTINUEMERGE : BOOLEAN;
    F,G,OUT : FILE OF INTEGER;
BEGIN
RESET(F); RESET(G); REWRITE(OUT);
CONTINUEMERGE := NOT(EOF(F) OR EOF(G));
WHILE CONTINUEMERGE DO
  BEGIN
  IF F↑ > G↑ THEN
    BEGIN
    OUT↑ := G↑; GET(G);
    CONTINUEMERGE ·:= NOT EOF(G)
    END
  ELSE
    BEGIN
    OUT↑ := F↑; GET(F);
    CONTINUEMERGE := NOT EOF(F)
    END;
  PUT(OUT)
  END;
WHILE NOT EOF(F) DO
  BEGIN
  OUT↑ := F↑; PUT(OUT); GET(F)
  END;
WHILE NOT EOF(G) DO
  BEGIN
  OUT↑ := G↑; PUT(OUT); GET(G)
  END
END.
```

8.4

```
    REPEAT
      READ(CH)
    UNTIL (CH >= 'A') AND (CH <= 'Z');
```

8.5

```
    WHILE (INPUT↑ < 'A') OR (INPUT↑ > 'Z') DO GET(INPUT)
```

Problem A suitable scheme is

```
PROGRAM CURRENCY(INPUT,OUTPUT,COINS);
TYPE POSINT = 0..MAXINT;
VAR  COINS : FILE OF  REAL;
     COINVALUES : FILE OF POSINT;
     SMALLEST,POUNDS,VALUE,CONVERSIONRATE : REAL;
     MONEY,NUMBER,INTVALUE : POSINT;
BEGIN
(* CONVERT COINS TO MULTIPLES OF LEAST COIN *)
  (* FIND THE SMALLEST COIN - IT IS AT THE END *)
  (* CREATE A FILE OF INTEGER MULTIPLES OF THE
     SMALLEST COIN *)
(* READ THE CONVERSION RATE *)
(* PROCESS THE VALUES TO BE CONVERTED *)
WHILE NOT EOF DO
  BEGIN
  (* READ THE AMOUNT TO BE CONVERTED *)
  (* CALCULATE THE NEW AMOUNT AS A MULTIPLE OF THE
     SMALLEST DENOMINATION *)
  (* PRINT THE NEW AMOUNT CORRECTLY *)
  (* SCAN THE COINVALUES FILE FOR THE NECESSARY COINS *)
  WHILE NOT EOF(COINVALUES) DO
    BEGIN
    (* READ A COIN VALUE *)
    (* CALCULATE THE NUMBER REQUIRED *)
    IF NUMBER <> 0 THEN
      BEGIN
      (* PRINT THE NUMBER OF COINS AND THEIR CORRECT VALUE *)
      (* CALCULATE THE AMOUNT REMAINING *)
      END
    END
  END
END.
```

Chapter 9

9.1(a)

```
    { },
    {RED},{GREEN},{BLUE},
    {RED,GREEN},{RED,BLUE},{GREEN,BLUE},
    {RED,GREEN,BLUE}
```

(b)

{ },
{1}, {2}, {3}, {4},
{1,2}, {1,3}, {1,4}, {2,3}, {2,4}, {3,4},
{1,2,3}, {1,2,4}, {1,3,4}, {2,3,4},
{1,2,3,4}

9.2(a)   [3]
(b)   [1 .. 5]
(c)   [1,2,4]

9.3(a)   TRUE   **(b)** TRUE   (c) FALSE   (d) FALSE

Chapter 10

10.1

```
PROGRAM FREQCOUNT(F,OUTPUT);
TYPE FREQ = ARRAY['A'..'Z'] OF 0..MAXINT;
VAR CH : CHAR;
    F : TEXT;
    COUNT : FREQ;
BEGIN
FOR CH := 'A' TO 'Z' DO COUNT[CH] := 0;
RESET(F);
WHILE NOT EOF(F) DO
  BEGIN
  READ(F,CH);
  IF CH IN ['A'..'Z'] THEN
    COUNT[CH] := COUNT[CH] + 1
  END
END.
```

10.2   Assuming that most combinations will occur, a suitable type would be

```
TYPE ALLTWOS = ARRAY[CHAR,CHAR] OF BOOLEAN;
```

Problem 10.2   The correct data structure is

```
TYPE PAIRFREQ = ARRAY['A'..'Z','A'..'Z'] OF 0..MAXINT;
```

A suitable scheme for the frequency calculation is

```
(* INITIALISE THE COUNTS TO ZERO *)
RESET(F);
IF NOT EOF(F) THEN (* READ THE FIRST CHARACTER *)
WHILE NOT EOF(F) DO
  BEGIN
  (* READ A SECOND CHARACTER *)
  IF (* BOTH CHARACTERS ARE LETTERS *) THEN
      (* INCREMENT THE FREQUENCY COUNT *)
  (* MAKE THE SECOND CHARACTER THE FIRST ONE *)
  END
END.
```

Chapter 11

11.1

```
FUNCTION DIFFERENCE(D1,D2 : DATE) : INTEGER;
  FUNCTION DAYSFROM1900(D : DATE) : INTEGER;
  VAR YEARS : 0..100;
      DAYS : 0..MAXINT;
      M : MONTH;
      DINYEAR : ARRAY[MONTH] OF 0..365;
  BEGIN (* DAYS FROM 1900 *)
  DINYEAR[JAN] := 0;   DINYEAR[FEB] := 31;  DINYEAR[MAR] := 59;
  DINYEAR[APR] := 90;  DINYEAR[MAY] := 120; DINYEAR[JUN] := 151;
  DINYEAR[JLY] := 181; DINYEAR[AUG] := 212; DINYEAR[SEP] := 243;
  DINYEAR[OCT] := 273; DINYEAR[NOV] := 304; DINYEAR[DEC] := 334;
  WITH D DO
    BEGIN
    YEARS := Y - 1900;
    DAYS := YEARS * 365;
    IF M <= FEB THEN YEARS := YEARS - 1;
    DAYS := DAYS + YEARS DIV 4;
    DAYS := DAYS + DINYEAR[M];
    DAYSFROM1900 := DAYS + D
    END
  END; (* DAYS FROM 1900 *)
BEGIN (* DIFFERENCE *)
DIFFERENCE := DAYSFROM1900(D2) - DAYSFROM1900(D1)
END; (* DIFFERENCE *)
```

11.2 Two changes are needed to the program. The first deals with the players'
names. A simple modification to the loop which reads a player's name will allow
the actual length of the name to be calculated. This information can be used to
control the output when the name is printed. The second modification produces
the longer description of the card. This requires the use of mapping functions or

CASE statements, one for card suits and one for card faces. **CASE** statements are preferable in both instances.

Problem A suitable data structure is:

```
TYPE MORSETABLE =
          ARRAY[CHAR] OF RECORD
                           VALID : BOOLEAN;
                           LENGTH : 1..6;
                           CODE : PACKED ARRAY[1..6] OF CHAR
                           END;
```

This is filled with the information from the file to provide a mapping from characters to their Morse code equivalents.

Chapter 12

12.1

```
FUNCTION PERIMETER(FIG : GEOMETRICFIGURE) : REAL;
CONST PI = 3.141596536;
BEGIN
WITH FIG DO
  CASE KIND OF
    RECT : PERIMETER := 2 * (HEIGHT + WIDTH);
    CIRC : PERIMETER := 2 * PI * RADIUS;
    TRI  : PERIMETER := SIDE1 + SIDE2 + SQRT(SQR(SIDE1) + SQR(SI
                        - 2 * SIDE1 * SIDE2 * COS(ANGLE))
  END
END; (* PERIMETER *)
```

12.2(a)

```
PROGRAM ANS122A(GIRLS,OUTPUT);
CONST N = 10;
TYPE STRING = PACKED ARRAY[1..N] OF CHAR;
     FULLNAME = RECORD
                     SURNAME : STRING;
                     NOOFFNAMES : 1..3;
                     FORENAMES : ARRAY[1..3] OF STRING
                     END;
     FEMALESTUDENT = RECORD
                          NAME : FULLNAME;
                          SIZE : ARRAY[1..3] OF 400..1299
                          END;
VAR GIRLS : FILE OF FEMALESTUDENT;
    AVSIZE : ARRAY[1..3] OF 0..MAXINT;
    I : 1..3;
    COUNT : 0..MAXINT;
    PERSON : FEMALESTUDENT;
BEGIN
RESET(GIRLS); COUNT := 0;
FOR I := 1 TO 3 DO AVSIZE[I] := 0;
WHILE NOT EOF(GIRLS) DO
  BEGIN
  READ(GIRLS,PERSON);
  WITH PERSON DO
    FOR I := 1 TO 3 DO
      AVSIZE[I] := AVSIZE[I] + SIZE[I];
  COUNT := COUNT + 1
  END;
IF COUNT = 0 THEN WRITE('EMPTY FILE')
ELSE
  FOR I := 1 TO 3 DO WRITE(AVSIZE[I] DIV COUNT);
WRITELN
END.
```

(b)

```pascal
PROGRAM ANS122B(MEN,OUTPUT);
CONST N = 10;
TYPE STRING = PACKED ARRAY[1..N] OF CHAR;
     FULLNAME = RECORD
                     SURNAME : STRING;
                     NOOFFNAMES : 1..3;
                     FORENAMES : ARRAY[1..3] OF STRING
                     END;
     MALESTUDENT = RECORD
                     NAME : FULLNAME;
                     MONEY : REAL;
                     CAR : BOOLEAN
                     END;
VAR MEN : FILE OF MALESTUDENT;
    CAROWNERS : 0..MAXINT;
    PERSON : MALESTUDENT;
    TOTAL : REAL;
    COUNT : 0..MAXINT;
BEGIN
CAROWNERS := 0; TOTAL := 0; COUNT := 0;
RESET(MEN);
WHILE NOT EOF(MEN) DO
  BEGIN
  READ(MEN,PERSON);
  WITH PERSON DO
    BEGIN
    IF CAR THEN CAROWNERS := CAROWNERS + 1;
    (* OR CAROWNERS := CAROWNERS + ORD(CAR) *)
    TOTAL := TOTAL + MONEY;
    COUNT := COUNT + 1
    END
  END;
IF COUNT = 0 THEN WRITELN('EMPTY FILE ')
ELSE WRITELN(CAROWNERS,TOTAL / COUNT)
END.
```

12.3

```
PROGRAM ANS123(CSSTUDENTS,OUTPUT);
CONST N = 10;
TYPE STRING = PACKED ARRAY[1..N] OF CHAR;
     FULLNAME = RECORD
                   SURNAME : STRING;
                   NOOFFNAMES : 1..3;
                   FORENAMES : ARRAY[1..3] OF STRING
                   END;
     SEX = (FEMALE,MALE);
     STUDENT = RECORD
                   NAME : FULLNAME;
                   CASE S : SEX OF
                      MALE    : (MONEY : REAL; CAR : BOOLEAN);
                      FEMALE : (SIZE : ARRAY[1..3] OF 400..1299)
                   END;
VAR MCOUNT,FCOUNT,CAROWNERS : 0..MAXINT;
    I : 1..3;
    TOTAL : REAL;
    AVSIZE : ARRAY[1..3] OF 0..MAXINT;
    PERSON : STUDENT;
    CSSTUDENTS : FILE OF STUDENT;
BEGIN
RESET(CSSTUDENTS);
MCOUNT := 0; FCOUNT := 0; TOTAL := 0;
CAROWNERS := 0;
FOR I := 1 TO 3 DO AVSIZE[I]:= 0;
WHILE NOT EOF(CSSTUDENTS) DO
  BEGIN
  READ(CSSTUDENTS,PERSON);
  WITH PERSON DO
    CASE S OF
       MALE    : BEGIN
                 IF CAR THEN CAROWNERS := CAROWNERS + 1;
                 TOTAL := TOTAL + MONEY;
                 MCOUNT := MCOUNT + 1
                 END;
       FEMALE : BEGIN
                 FOR I := 1 TO 3 DO
                    AVSIZE[I] := AVSIZE[I] + SIZE[I];
                 FCOUNT := FCOUNT + 1
                 END
    END
  END;
IF MCOUNT = 0 THEN WRITELN('NO MALES')
ELSE WRITELN(CAROWNERS,TOTAL / MCOUNT);
IF FCOUNT = 0 THEN WRITE('NO FEMALES')
ELSE
  FOR I := 1 TO 3 DO WRITE(AVSIZE[I] DIV FCOUNT);
WRITELN
END.
```

Chapter 13

13.1

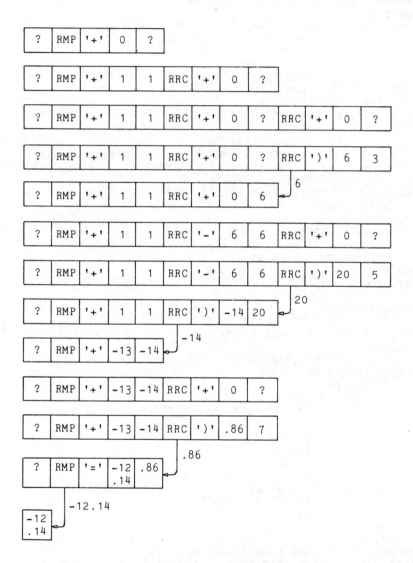

```
where   RMP means Return to Main Program
and     RRC means Return to Recursive Call
```

13.2

```
FUNCTION POS(FUNCTION F : REAL) : BOOLEAN;
    VAR X : REAL;
    BEGIN
    X := -0.1;
    REPEAT
        X := X + 0.1
    UNTIL (X > 0.95) OR ( F(X) < 0);
    POS := F(X) < 0
    END;
```

Problem

```
PROCEDURE TRY(I : INTEGER);
    BEGIN
    initialise selection of positions
        for I-th queen;
    REPEAT
        make next selection;
        IF safe THEN
            BEGIN
            setqueen;
            IF I < 8 THEN
                BEGIN
                TRY(I + 1);
                IF NOT SUCCESSFULL THEN
                    remove queen
                END
            END
    UNTIL SUCCESSFULL OR no more positions
    END;
```

Chapter 14

14.1   At the beginning of step 4 add

W := **NIL**;

Just before using W in the statement

W↑.COSTFIXED := TRUE;

a test can be inserted to see if W equals **NIL**. If so, an error message can be produced and the program terminated.

14.2   A dummy header will be needed as well as a sentinel (see Wirth, 1975*b*, chapter 4). The change does not significantly alter the performance of the program.

14.3

```
PROCEDURE PRINTROUTE(DEST : PNODE);
TYPE PROUTE = ↑ROUTEITEM;
     ROUTEITEM = RECORD
                     PTR : PNODE;
                     NEXT : PROUTE
                     END;
VAR P : PNODE;
    RLIST,R : PROUTE;
BEGIN
WRITELN(' THE BEST ROUTE IS ');
P := DEST; RLIST := NIL;
WHILE P <> NIL DO
  BEGIN
  NEW(R);
  R↑.PTR := P;
  R↑.NEXT := RLIST;
  RLIST := R;
  P := P↑.MINTOHERE
  END;
WHILE RLIST <> NIL DO
  BEGIN
  WRITELN(RLIST↑.PTR↑.NAME);
  R := RLIST;
  RLIST := RLIST↑.NEXT;
  DISPOSE(R)
  END
END; (* OF PRINTROUTE *)
```

14.4 A suitable data structure is a linked list of records, which are used to form a sequence of the members of the set. The members of the set should be kept in (ascending) order in the sequence to facilitate the programming of the set operations. For further details, see the references in chapter 9.

Appendix IV The Pascal User's Group

The Pascal User's Group (PUG) has been formed to promote the use of the programming language Pascal as well as the ideas behind it. The following information is taken from *Pascal News*, the official but *informal* publication of the User's Group. Generally produced four times during an academic year— September, November, February, May—the contents of *Pascal News* include: policy, editor's contribution, 'here and there with Pascal', articles, open forum for members, implementation notes. Membership of PUG can be arranged through the following addresses.

Pascal User's Group
c/o Andy Mickel
University Computer Center
208 SE Union Street
University of Minnesota
Minneapolis, MN 55455
USA

Pascal User's Group (UK)
c/o Computer Studies Group
Mathematics Department
The University
Southampton SO9 5NH
United Kingdom

Pascal User's Group (AUS)
c/o Arthur Sale
Dept of Information Science
University of Tasmania
GPO Box 252C
Hobart, Tasmania 7001
Australia

The Programming Language Pascal

Addyman, A. M., *et al.* (1979), A draft description of Pascal, *Pascal News*, 14, and *Software Practice and Experience*, 9,4.

Habermann, A. N. (1974), Critical comments on the programming language Pascal, *Acta Informatica*, 3, 47-57.

Hoare, C. A. R., and Wirth, N. (1973), An axiomatic definition of the programming language Pascal, *Acta Informatica*, 2, 335-55.

Jensen, K., and Wirth, N. (1975), *Pascal-User Manual and Report* (Springer-Verlag, New York).

Lecarme, O., and Desjardins, P. (1975), More comments on the programming language Pascal, *Acta Informatica*, 4, 231-43.

Pascal News (formerly *Pascal Newsletter*), all issues.

Welsh, J., Sneeringer, W. J., and Hoare, C. A. R. (1977), Ambiguities and insecurities in Pascal, *Software Practice and Experience*, 7, 685-96.

Wirth, N. (1975a), An assessment of the programming language Pascal, *SIGPLAN Notices*, 10, 23-30.

Programming

Aho, A. V., Hopcroft, J. E., and Ullman, J. D. (1974), *The Design and Analysis of Computer Algorithms* (Addison-Wesley, Reading, Mass.).

Coleman, D. (1978), *A Structured Programming Approach to Data* (Macmillan, London and Basingstoke).

Computing Surveys (1974), 6, part 4 (complete issue).

Dahl, O. J., Dijkstra, E. W., and Hoare, C. A. R. (1972), *Structured Programming* (Academic Press, New York).

Knuth, D. (1973), *The Art of Computer Programming*, 3 vols (Addison-Wesley, Reading, Mass.).

Page, E. S., and Wilson, L. B. (1973), *Information Representation and Manipulation in a Computer* (Cambridge University Press).

Wirth, N. (1971), Program development by step-wise refinement, *Communs ACM*, 14, 221-27.

Wirth, N. (1975b), *Algorithms + Data Structures = Programs* (Prentice-Hall, Englewood Cliffs, N.J.).

Algebra

Gill, Arthur (1976), *Applied Algebra for the Computer Sciences* (Prentice-Hall, Englewood Cliffs, N.J.).

Symbol and Word Index